D0053272

The Trayvon Generation

The Trayvon Generation

Elizabeth Alexander

GRAND CENTRAL
PUBLISHING

NEW YORK   BOSTON

Grand Central Publishing
Hachette Book Group
1290 Avenue of the Americas, New York, NY 10104
grandcentralpublishing.com
twitter.com/grandcentralpub

First Edition: April 2022

Grand Central Publishing is a division of Hachette Book Group, Inc. The Grand Central Publishing name and logo is a trademark of Hachette Book Group, Inc.

The publisher is not responsible for websites (or their content) that are not owned by the publisher.

The Hachette Speakers Bureau provides a wide range of authors for speaking events. To find out more, go to www.hachettespeakersbureau.com or call (866) 376-6591.

Additional copyright and credits information are on pages 139–144.

Library of Congress Cataloging-in-Publication Data has been applied for.
Names: Alexander, Elizabeth, author.
Title: The Trayvon generation / Elizabeth Alexander.
Description: First edition. | New York, NY : Grand Central Publishing, 2022.
Identifiers: LCCN 2021041296 | ISBN 9781538737897 (hardcover) |
    ISBN 9781538737903 (ebook)
Subjects: LCSH: African Americans—Social conditions. | African American youth—
    Psychology. | African American mothers—Psychology. | African Americans—
    Crimes against. | Martin, Trayvon, 1995–2012—Influence. | Race discrimination—
    United States. | Racism—United States.
Classification: LCC E185.86 .A37945 2022 | DDC 305.896/073—dc23
LC record available at https://lccn.loc.gov/2021041296

ISBN: 9781538737897 (hardcover), 9781538737903 (ebook)

Printed in the United States of America

WOR

10 9 8 7 6 5 4 3 2 1

Again, for Solo, Simon, Robel, Maurice,
Cameron, and Sekou,
and their brave and beautiful generation

Jennifer Packer
Blessed Are Those Who Mourn (Breonna! Breonna!), 2020

Contents

I

"what will be the sacred words?"   3

"here lies"   13

"shock of delayed comprehension"   27

a tale of two textbooks   39

"cemetery for the illustrious negro dead"   48

II

the trayvon generation   67

III

"we dress our ideas in clothes to make the
        abstract visible"   85

"whether the negro sheds tears"   101

"there are black people in the future"   108

Acknowledgments	131
Notes	133
Credits	139
About the Author	145

PART I

Lorna Simpson
Thin Bands (detail), 2019

"what will be the sacred words?"

The problem of the twenty-first century remains the color line. Yes, we are mired in overlapping societal struggles and challenges. But white supremacy and its many manifestations—some of them sly and cloaked, some of them clear as a Confederate flag flown by marauders in the US Capitol—has been a fundamental problem for every generation in this country since Black people first came to this land. W. E. B. Du Bois's "How does it feel to be a problem?" is still the question implicitly and explicitly directed at Black people. The race work of the generations of my great-grandparents, my grandparents, my parents, and myself is the work of our children's generation. I don't wring my hands that "we didn't fix it"; clearly it is unfixable by us alone. White supremacy is not the creation of Black people. I both lament and am enraged that this work is undone, and that our young people still have it to wrestle with.

Racial ideologies are insidious. They instruct in intricate, ambient teaching systems. The country is their classroom and everyone is in school, whether they choose to be or not. Thus the color line is a fundamental, formative, constitutive American problem.

I was raised in troves of blackness: born in a Black metropolis, Harlem USA; reared in Chocolate City, Washington, D.C., which, in my childhood, was nearly three-quarters Black.[1] From my family, I was given a sense of pride in our people and history, the need to understand myself as part of a larger whole and to be as helpful as I could to others, the familiar imperative to work "twice as hard," and the responsibility to speak up when injustice was done.

When I found my professional path, it was as an educator, a scholar of Black culture, and an organizer of words, mostly poems. I wrote and thought and taught about the importance of witnessing; about the crucial functions of storytelling and history; about how the specter of violence hangs as constantly as the moon over Black people. I found knowledge and guidance in words, and possibilities in music, dance, and art, where I could go outside of words and access feeling and deep knowing. In Black history and culture, I encountered the full range of human experience, conundrum, perseverance, beauty, foible, and particularity. Here everything could be understood and I evangelized in my teaching and writing about this wellspring.

I believed that representation mattered, and that if more of "us" occupied spaces where justice-minded decisions could be made, power shared, and examples set, "the race" could move forward and, with that, all of society would strengthen itself and mend the corrosion of ignorance and racism.

Here is the thorny truth: while many sectors of society are now more integrated, violence and fear are unabated, and the war against Black people feels as if it is gearing up for another epic round.

This poem by Clint Smith gets to the perennialness and sorrow of race in America:

Your National Anthem

Today, a black man who was once a black boy
like you got down on one of his knees & laid
his helmet on the grass as this country sang

its ode to the promise it never kept
& the woman in the grocery store line in front
of us is on the phone & she is telling someone

on the other line that this black man who was
once a black boy like you should be grateful
we live in a country where people aren't killed

for things like this you know she says, in some places
they would hang you for such a blatant act of
    disrespect
maybe he should go live there instead of here so
    he can

appreciate what he has & then she turns around
& sees you sitting in the grocery cart surrounded
by lettuce & yogurt & frozen chicken thighs

& you smile at her with your toothless gum smile
& she says that you are the cutest baby she has
ever seen & tells me how I must feel so lucky

to have such a beautiful baby boy & I thank her
for her kind words even though I should not
thank her because I know that you will not always

be a black boy but one day you may be a black man
& you may decide your country hasn't kept
its promise to you either & this woman or another

like her will forget that you were ever this boy &
   they
will make you into something else & tell you
to be grateful for what you've been given

The small word *may* is the devastation in this poem.
In the scene at a supermarket, the precious Black boy—
the speaker's son—is admired by a white woman who
in the same breath decries the actions of a Black man
asking better of his country, as we always have; she
upends his belonging—that baby, in the words of his
father, may grow up to "be a black man." Not *will* but *may*
grow up.

Racial violence exists on a long continuum, and we
refuse to understand that at our peril. Though I may
worry in particular ways about my own sons as do other
parents of Black children, this is a worry that we all must
share. When human beings look at other human beings in
their midst and instead of seeing other human beings see
a threat, see something monstrous, or don't see at all, our
very humanity is at stake.

Layered atop the never-ending anxiety of parenting,
Black parents live with the truth that we cannot fully

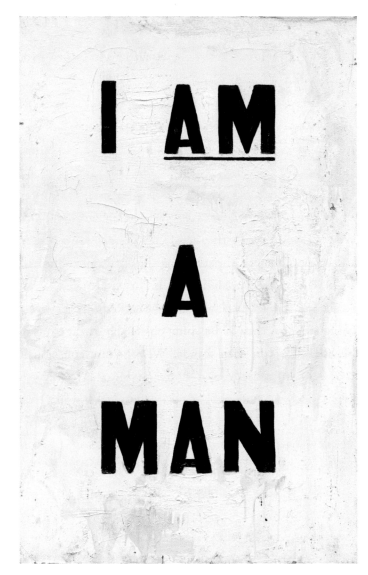

Glenn Ligon
Untitled (I Am A Man), 1988

protect our children. As a people, we have lived with too much suffering, and we live among many others who do not go through life with the same degree of precarity and loss. When yet another young Black person is shot dead— in their neighborhood, while jogging, in their bed—we brace in anticipation of the tableaux to come: the neighborhood funeral, the raw grief of mothers, the unlikelihood of a trial, and, if a trial, the character assault on the person who was murdered—they were out too late, they were in the street and not on the sidewalk, they had smoked a little weed, they passed a counterfeit bill, they dangled an air freshener from the back window, they asked why they were being stopped, they had a shiny object that turned out to be house keys in their hands. We who live consciously in this reality stay distracted and anxious, those feelings heightened when there is a trial and our faith is tested once again, and our children feel no safer. Our anxiety may even stifle the joy and exuberance that should characterize their childhood.

In addition to the crisis of violence against people of color, we are at the outer edge of an era of a crisis wherein speech has been debased from the highest levels of governance, and abusive language and its violence are increasingly ambient. Words are vessels filled with meaning and intent. Our language is what we live in, and thus how we collectively express ourselves, one voice at a time. If we believe in the power of words, and that words matter, and that precision with words matters most; and if we believe that words not only carry meaning but also carry something human, that shared language and the exchange of language are among the things that make us human; and if we believe that striving for absolute truth with the word is one of the ways that human beings can communicate deeply enough in order to overcome that which is not understood between us; if we believe also that there is too much language in the air right now that is imprecise, false, harmful, operating not to bridge understanding but to create misunderstanding, to divide, and that there is very precise if inelegant language that is being used for the purpose of misnaming and dividing us; then we might ask: What is the power of our words? How are we responsible for them? What can we do with them, and do words move us closer to the hoped-for ideal of beloved community?

Language is one of the ways we share our perspectives, our very selves, and one of the zones of hope I have for reaching across the voids between us. I do not mean to suggest that talk and explication are a solution. Indeed, the burden of explaining has always been hoisted on Black shoulders, and it has not solved the fundamental problem. Black people did not create the problem; it's a great societal head fake to look to us to solve problems not of our making and behaviors not of our doing.

But for all of us, language is how we say who we are, and we cannot solve our problems without it. Language is one of the few media with which to make conundrums visible and solutions tangible. Language is how we learn across difference. And language is in trouble.

Poets especially use words in ways that are visceral and remind us in the best of poems that they are products of the human body. People, and peoples, tell their stories to each other; the tribe needs to chronicle itself. Human beings in all cultures across time have yielded to the impulse to make song. A poem is physically a small thing, but it has the density and potency that in the best cases is a force forever.

In Black culture, our poetry sometimes holds and memorializes our history. Amid insufficient memorializing and in the face of scant or buried histories, Black poets have made experience solid and enduring in too many examples to count. Black poetry remembers, and Black poetry memorializes. Poems are how we say, *This is who we are*, how we chronicle ourselves when we are insufficiently found in history books and commemorative sites. And as with monuments, the poem outlasts the poet.

The times stay challenging and our society urgently needs repair. The fundamental proposition and question that arises at the end of the poem "Ka 'Ba" by Amiri Baraka, published in 1969, continues to resonate:

> We need magic
> now we need the spells, to raise up
> return, destroy, and create. What will be
>
> the sacred words?

I hear it in my head most days: *What will be the sacred words?*

"here lies"

Monuments and memorials ask that we remember those who have died and make permanent what they stand for: individuals, communities, ideas. The word *remember* has a physicality to it—re-member—the idea that without remembrance the corpus of the person or people or place or idea or ideology has been physically torn asunder.

The American monument landscape teaches us many things, the greatest of which is that Black people are inferior to white people. No other people in the United States are so extensively portrayed in a built public history that asserts their subhumanity and teaches the superiority of others. For example, Confederate public symbols continue to predominate in the US: monuments and statues, government buildings, plaques, markers, schools, parks, counties, cities, military property, and streets and highways named after anyone associated with the Confederacy. Many public schools—often with large Black student populations—are still named for Robert E. Lee, Jefferson Davis, and other Confederate icons. There are sixty-four counties and cities named for Confederates, twelve US military bases named for Confederates, and twenty-five official Confederate holidays in eleven states.[2]

Other memorials and monuments besides the Confederate assert and justify dominion and subjugation. The recently removed statue of Theodore Roosevelt outside New York's American Museum of Natural History comes to mind, with Roosevelt elevated high on horseback with half-clothed Black and Native American men flanking him below. Another is the recently removed statue of Dr. J. Marion Sims in East Harlem. He was known as "the father of gynecology" and made his name through brutal experimental surgeries performed on enslaved Black women against their will and without benefit of anesthesia.[3] What were these statues teaching the many, many passersby about who is fully human and deserving of basic respect?

It is important to note that almost none of the Confederate monuments and statues actually date from the Civil War. They were put up in the decades following, to express and instantiate the ideology of white supremacy.

Their dedication and rededication especially flourished during the first two decades of the twentieth century and during the Civil Rights Movement—more than forty-five between the US Supreme Court's *Brown v. Board of Education* school desegregation decision in 1954 and the assassination of Dr. Martin Luther King Jr. in 1968.[4] And over forty-nine monuments and other symbols have been dedicated or rededicated since 2000.[5]

I am finally beginning to fully understand the didactic violence of monuments and what they revere and hold up as glorious. Their relative scale, too, instructs, as in the famous 1569 world map made by the cartographer Gerardus Mercator that distorts Europe and North America to a size far larger than Africa or Latin America. Its orientation and scale tell us a lie about the world and its inhabitants. Is the continent of Africa larger than Greenland? In fact, Greenland is the same size as the Democratic Republic of the Congo, but one country among the fifty-four on the entire vast continent. Is Europe bigger than South America? Does the United States sit at the center of the world? Is there a center of the world? Maps are not neutral. Maps are not, inherently, "true." Maps have points of view. Maps carry cultural bias. Maps tell stories. The Mercator projection was embraced long after its original semiaccurate navigation had expired, and the map's distortions were seldom pointed out in the many classrooms where world maps hung. Rather, it was presented as the full, straightforward truth, and we live with that map even today.

Monuments put forth ideas and look forward, even when their content is historical. They chart future values by what they revere. How African Americans themselves remember, and remember in shared and accessible spaces has been the powerful mission of Black poets and artists, and those spaces are where we have held our history and shown who and what we venerate. The aspiration or ambition to be remembered, to be present in the landscape, to cast a shadow, to be immortal—these are not the values of men and white people alone. But I do think a zero-sum game of American storytelling suggests that history moves along a single line, that we can know it all, know everything and everyone. Rather, many things can be true at once.

When Lucille Clifton was named poet laureate of the state of Maryland—the state where Harriet Tubman was born in bondage and escaped slavery and from where she led groups of enslaved people to liberty in Canada an estimated thirteen times; and where Frederick Douglass was

Mary Sibande
The Reign, 2010

born and was said to look out from the porch of his home in Anacostia to the ocean waves that marked where he was born enslaved and then, to measure his life, toward downtown Washington, D.C., where he served as a US diplomat—she was asked to write a poem on the topic "celebrating our colonial heritage" for the state's 350th anniversary.[6] This was her response:

why some people be mad at me sometimes

they ask me to remember
but they want me to remember
their memories
and i keep on remembering
mine.

The Black vernacular title is in sharp contrast to the euphemistic, standard English of "our colonial heritage." To use a favorite Clifton adjective, an "ordinary" Black woman is speaking back in this poem. "Some people" are not named; they need not be named; they are "some" people, more than one, more than once, unworthy of naming.

She refuses to replicate the mythology of "our colonial heritage" in the poem. Clifton is simultaneously frontal and subversive. She stands in the interregnum between the old order and the new and overwrites an ideology that would dare continue to teach that anyone was inferior or superior to anyone else. In "why some people" she essentially says, *They keeping telling lies about history, and I refuse and refute.* The poem itself becomes a monument. Lucille Clifton is one of poetry's great meditators on history in small, essential forms.

Clifton "keep[s] on remembering," telling the truth, bearing witness to history itself, the stories and names otherwise lost, distorted, or minimized. The simple questions of whose bodies and histories are beneath our feet and how the earth speaks to us are explored in this poem:

at the cemetery, walnut grove plantation, south carolina, 1989

among the rocks
at walnut grove
your silence drumming

in my bones,
tell me your names.

nobody mentioned slaves
and yet the curious tools
shine with your fingerprints.
nobody mentioned slaves
but somebody did this work
who had no guide, no stone,
who moulders under rock.

tell me your names,
tell me your bashful names
and I will testify.

the inventory lists ten slaves
but only men were recognized.

among the rocks
at walnut grove
some of these honored dead
were dark
some of these dark
were slaves
some of these slaves

were women
some of them did this honored work.
tell me your names
foremothers, brothers,
tell me your dishonored names.
here lies
here lies
here lies
here lies
hear

Here lies marks the location of bodies, and the stories told and untold. *Here lies* are ritual words spoken at a burial, a formally elevated sentence opening that ordinarily would be followed by a name, and then a person would be spoken of with honor. But Clifton repeats the phrase four times; we repeat as blessing and invocation. The phrase also falls apart with repetition and becomes not the ceremonial opening but rather the "lies" that justify the existence of slavery and white supremacy. The final word, a line unto itself, *hear*, moves the specificity of the location to the imperative to listen to what the land and its people tell us.

The Confederate Memorial Carving at Stone Mountain

Park in Georgia is the largest bas-relief sculpture on Earth and has been called "the largest shrine to white supremacy in the history of the world."[7] It is forty-five feet deep, looms four hundred feet tall, and took fifty-seven years to complete. The memorial renders in stone three Confederate heroes: Jefferson Davis, Robert E. Lee, and Thomas "Stonewall" Jackson. It is bigger than Mount Rushmore and leaves everything before it in shadow.

Stone Mountain has deep ties to the Ku Klux Klan: the first of its three sculptors was a member of the KKK, Klan

Kara Walker

money aided in the monument's original funding, and the owner of the mountain into which the sculpture was carved was also a Klansman. In 1915, the Klan held a revival meeting on top of the mountain, and KKK meetings continued in that location for decades.[8] Today, it looms over field trips by local schools, concerts, and other community events. To face Stone Mountain is to be small in its presence, to feel awe, and, if you read its messages, to feel fear.

Artist Kara Walker was born in 1969 and was raised almost literally in the shadow of Stone Mountain. Much

The Jubilant Martyrs of Obsolescence and Ruin, 2015

of her work can be read as a response, corrective, and resistance to the undying violent white supremacist ideology she grew up in in the built environment that dominated her view. Indeed she says that Stone Mountain is the biggest influence on her art.[9] Her work explores the societal psychosis that white supremacy produces and how racism corrodes and deforms everything it touches.

The High Museum of Art in Atlanta acquired Walker's *The Jubilant Martyrs of Obsolescence and Ruin*, a sixty-foot work of her signature cutouts that stands as a rejoinder to Stone Mountain and its logic. It essentially faces the mountain, and it exposes what the mountain teaches, both engaging and overwriting its assertions, as eternal as the mountain.

The poet Adrienne Su's parents came to greater Atlanta as immigrants from China, and she writes about how Stone Mountain was normalized in her childhood.

Personal History

The world's largest Confederate monument
was too big to perceive on my earliest trips to the park.
Unlike my parents, I was not an immigrant

but learned, in speech and writing, to represent.
Picnicking at the foot and sometimes peak
of the world's largest Confederate monument,

we raised our Cokes to the first Georgian president.
His daughter was nine like me, but Jimmy Carter,
unlike my father, was not an immigrant.

Teachers and tour guides stressed the achievement
of turning three vertical granite acres into art.
Since no one called it a Confederate monument,

it remained invisible, like outdated wallpaper
    meant
long ago to be stripped. Nothing at Stone Mountain
    Park
echoed my ancestry, but it's normal for immigrants

not to see themselves in landmarks. On summer
    nights,
fireworks and laser shows obscured, with sparks,
the world's largest Confederate monument.
Our story began when my parents arrived as
    immigrants.

The looming dominance of Stone Mountain was such that its white supremacy "remained invisible" as its "achievement" was lauded in school. And for the immigrant who was neither white nor Black, Stone Mountain was a lesson in white hegemony. We would later see this echoed in the wave of epithets and violence against Asian Americans that erupted in the later days of the global COVID-19 pandemic. A white man who frequented Atlanta massage parlors went on a killing spree and murdered eight people, six of whom were Asian American women who worked in such spas. Their dehumanization in the stereotype of compliant women available for sex was a precedent to their killing. Dehumanization precedes violence—in fact, is a precondition for it.

And so it begins with history, and its still-embattled landscape.

"shock of delayed comprehension"

The Corporation Room at Yale is where the most important meetings at the university are held. From time to time over the fifteen years that I was a professor and department chair, I would enter it for meetings such as a presidential committee on admissions or when special visitors came to the university. I came to the room with a sense of occasion, carefully prepared, and did my work.

At the end of the room was a portrait of Yale's namesake, Elihu Yale. It was like so many portraits of Yale-related men across the centuries: frontal, formal, ubiquitous. In those years I didn't expect there to be images of people of color, or women, even though it gnawed at me that there weren't. I would conduct my business, and Elihu Yale would preside from his wall space at the head of the room.

Once on a college break I went to Howard University in my home of Washington, D.C., to work in Founders

Library and the Moorland-Spingarn Research Center. The research holdings in African American culture were extraordinary, and I was eager to explore them. I had never before been on the campus of this Black school; I'd spent time on the surrounding streets but had never walked through the gates. At Howard as at Yale, there was a formal feel in the portraits on the wall, a similar imbalanced ratio of men to women. But these men were mostly Black. The script had been flipped. The students too were flipped: Howard was a "traditional"-looking campus, all Black. From my childhood, the feeling of being almost fully among Black people and at home was not new to me. I didn't consider it being in the majority, I considered it the norm. It was the city, my city, and I loved Lucille Clifton's words: "in the inner city / or / like we called it / home."[10] But this visit to Howard made me think for the first time about what it meant to attend a school where women and people of color were near-invisible.

Back to my time on the Yale faculty, many years later, in that conference room. One day, for no particular reason, I looked at the painting again and saw what I had never once noticed: in the painting *Elihu Yale with his Servant* was a diminutive brown-skinned figure with a highly polished metal collar around his neck at the foot of the university's namesake. The brown-skinned figure's outfit suggests that he is Indian or South Asian, but neither his racial identity nor age is clear. What is certain is the collar, which signals his status as property. In the symbolic landscape of the painting, he is a representation of Elihu Yale's wealth and power—in line with Yale's involvement with the slave trade and the East India Company, although he may not have owned slaves himself.[11] The servant/slave is unnamed and unknown. I had not focused on the discomfiting scene in all those years in that room. Or perhaps I had erased it from my mind, because the implications of the whole story of the picture and its placement in a space of honor would have opened a cascade of questions and conundrums.

To return for a moment to Stone Mountain, Adrienne Su offers us a useful concept about its childhood influence:

> ...my own memories of it include hiking up the trail on the back of the mountain, setting out a blanket to watch a laser show, and walking among the goldfish ponds at the mountain's peak. When I learned the obvious (that the carving is the world's largest and perhaps

least erasable Confederate monument) as well as the less obvious (that the carving, begun in 1923, had stalled in 1928 but resumed in 1964 in response to *Brown v. Board of Education* and the Civil Rights Movement), I wanted to write about the shock of delayed comprehension.[12]

The shock of delayed comprehension. This phrase perfectly illustrates my experience in the Corporation Room at Yale. I had been sitting all those years not noticing. It was normal, normalized. And nobody seemed to notice.

Once I saw, I could not stop looking at the figure. I could barely conduct business as usual. *The shock of delayed comprehension.* What did it mean that I had not seen? I asked colleagues, *Did you see? Do you see? When did you notice?* Now that I saw and could not unsee, how much of my brain space was being taken up that could be used for other things? I did my work under the matter-of-fact, unproblematized image of an enslaved brown figure at the foot of the most venerated person in the university's history, our very namesake. How was I a part of this *we*?

As an undergraduate at Yale, it turns out that I had many encounters with a similar painting. Now titled *Elihu*

Yale with Members of his Family and an Enslaved Child, the group portrait once again centers Elihu Yale, this time with a small Black boy who is perhaps eight years old and wears a padlocked metal collar. In my college years in the early 1980s it was hung in Berkeley College's dining hall, where I frequently ate. I don't particularly remember noticing this enslaved Black boy then and now he haunts me.

A fellow Yale employee, Corey Menafee, took a different approach a few years later, in the dining room of the Yale residential college named for John C. Calhoun, a slave owner and famous defender of the institution of slavery. Working in the dining hall day after day, Menafee noticed what had been around him all the time when a Black alumnus came through with his daughter and pointed to the stained-glass windows portraying enslaved Black people picking cotton in the fields and smiling. The slaves in the image were happy.

"Like they say, a picture's worth a thousand words," said Menafee. He continued,

> That picture might have been worth a million words. I don't know, it just hit me. It just touched my heart to look up in 2016 and to see real— well, it was a picture, but a picture depicting real

slaves in a field picking cotton. There's no real place for that in today's society. It's degrading, it's disrespectful, and it shouldn't be there. Period.[13]

So soon thereafter Menafee picked up a broom and smashed out the stained-glass window.

These images are not just assaults to Black people. They say to the white people who are exposed to them over and over, all day every day, *This is normal. Slavery was normal.* By continuing to display it without comment or counter, we say yes to it. We venerate the man who displays his wealth by being painted with an enslaved figure. The picture teaches us that white supremacy is matter-of-fact, casual, and ordinary. It teaches that to all the nonwhite and non-Black people who see it. It teaches them that history does not need to be historicized—ironic, at a university that pioneered the idea that "all history is revisionist history." Leaving this painting hanging for so long and without comment had normalized its content. In a place of highest education, education was not happening.

These paintings have since been moved and, in the Corporation Room, replaced with another painting of Elihu Yale. The group portrait now hangs in the Yale Center for

Robert Pruitt
Up, Up, in the Upper Room, 2012

British Art and has been thoughtfully contextualized with contributions from historians and other scholars. Museum director Courtney J. Martin asks that viewers see what happens when they center the Black boy in their looking. The Calhoun stained glass has not yet been replaced. The university is taking a serious look at its campus and its representation in portraits of women and people of color. For example, in 2016, Titus Kaphar was invited to respond to Elihu Yale's portraits and created *Enough About You*, elevating and centering the young boy within a gold frame and crumpling the other figures behind him. Kaphar's piece was hung in place of the group portrait while it was being further researched. In 2019, Elizabeth Fitzsousa and Nientara Anderson—medical students at the time—and associate professor of medicine Anna Reisman published a report, *"This Institution Was Never Meant for Me": The Impact of Institutional Historical Portraiture on Medical Students*.[14] Therein they examined medical students' reactions to fifty-five portraits hanging in portions of the school's Sterling Hall of Medicine building, which depict three white women and fifty-two white men. The counting had never been done, nor the noticing, and nothing can change until that fundamental accounting takes place.

I have been thinking about the difference between evolution and revolution. Evolution moves forward in unfolding time, and over time, the organism changes. There is all the time in the world to catch up; that's evolution. Revolution is a sharp turn, an about-face, occasioning acceleration. Some things need to be done decisively and happen fast. Sometimes, places and people and ideas need to be jolted forward into the present tense so the organism can continue to grow and flourish. Both evolution and revolution have their place, time, and utility. But we don't move forward without moments when we take sharp turns into the future.

The first classes of undergraduate women to attend Yale graduated in 1971. Seeds had been planted earlier, with women who were pioneers in the graduate schools, like Pauli Murray and Grace Hopper. I am especially interested in Otelia Cromwell, who was the first Black woman to graduate from Smith College and the first Black woman to earn a PhD degree from both Yale and from an English Department anywhere, in 1926. She wrote a dissertation on Elizabethan drama, which was published by Yale University Press two years later; though her wish was to write about Black literature, she knew, as she wrote in a letter to her father on July 13, 1922, that any work which I might do in that line would be absolutely independent because, naturally, I'd know more about it than any of the folks here. In one way the independent work would show a certain kind of power, but on the other hand, my main object in being here is to learn scholarly method and to benefit by scholarly criticism. Most of all, I want the work I may do in the years to come—if years are granted me—to be critically sound.[15]

There isn't a lot on Cromwell in the Yale alumni files, but combing her graduate files for evidence of her time in that very record-keeping place, I found a letter she wrote on October 6, 1922, to the Yale Athletic Association, requesting two tickets for the Harvard–Yale game. "If I may have the privilege of buying tickets," she wrote, "will you send me an application blank?" It is noted for alumni records that she became a member of the board of directors who would have charge of an "encyclopedia of the negro," an important project of W. E. B. Du Bois's. From 1939 forward, her name is listed in a special card file labeled "Negroes Who Attended Yale," and in other places on the record, she is identified as "colored."[16]

Cromwell's example and history have always felt proximate to me because, since careers as professors in schools like Yale were not open to Black women when she earned her degree, she went on to teach at Dunbar High School, the renowned Black academic high school in Washington, D.C., where one of her students was my beloved grandmother, Wenonah Bond Logan. I grew up being trained and corrected in my grammar, word choice, and reading habits by my grandmother, who attributed every dictum to "Miss Otelia Cromwell."

When my classmates and I arrived on campus as undergraduates in 1980, it was amazing to us to think that the first class with women had graduated only a few years before. To ground us in that moment in time, Yale didn't have a woman department chair until six years before we came, nor a female provost. There still has not been a woman named president. The women's sports teams' captains' pictures were first placed on the walls of the campus club Mory's, and the women's studies major was approved in my sophomore year, despite the fact that an English professor submitted a mock proposal to the entire faculty referring to it as the "Department of Grossness" and questioning the field as an academic pursuit.[17] One of the things I used to speak of on campus as a professor and department chair was the legacy of Otelia Cromwell, and the importance of telling such stories as part of the history of the institution.

Today, there are not one but two portraits of Dr. Otelia Cromwell on Yale's campus, painted by two different Black women graduates of the art school, Jennifer Packer and Kenturah Davis. And as Yale students said in the 2015 Black Lives Matter protests that, among other things, agitated for a name change for Calhoun College, "We out here."[18] When those young people protested, they made a temporary cemetery on the college lawn with headstones of Black thinkers like Audre Lorde and James Baldwin whose ideas and actions challenged the ideology and legacy of white supremacy carried out by the likes of John Calhoun. The college has been renamed for Grace Hopper, a computer scientist and navy rear admiral who earned a PhD in mathematics from Yale in 1934. Corey Menafee was fired from Yale and then rehired later (at a different dining hall). The artist Faith Ringgold has been commissioned to put something new in the college. As with so many sites and communities, the future is a blank slate and an open door.

a tale of two textbooks

Textbooks are how most of us learn history, and the stakes are high for what is in them. In "Southern History," poet Natasha Trethewey describes a textbook she learned from as a schoolchild in the early 1970s in Mississippi:

Southern History

Before the war, they were happy, he said,
quoting our textbook. (This was senior-year

history class.) *The slaves were clothed, fed,
and better off under a master's care.*

I watched the words blur on the page. No one
raised a hand, disagreed. Not even me.

It was late; we still had Reconstruction
to cover before the test, and — luckily —

three hours of watching *Gone with the Wind*.
History, the teacher said, of the old South —

a true account of how things were back then.
On screen a slave stood big as life: big mouth,

bucked eyes, our textbook's grinning proof — a lie
my teacher guarded. Silent, so did I.

The child feels guilty for not rising to address the racism, as I felt guilty for not raising a ruckus over the portrait in the Corporation Room. "The slaves were clothed, fed, and better off under a master's care," the textbook read, and the Black child feels she is the one to fix it, even though she is not.

Assuming that parents across race believe that if their children have better textbooks and better teachers—especially in their civics and history courses—they would grow up to be better citizens, the textbook itself is an instrument for this logic. This is a tale of two textbooks by the great historian John Hope Franklin: the iconic *From Slavery to Freedom* and his lesser-known *Land of the Free*. Looking closely at the labor and context of writing both mainstream American history and Black history underscores the animating impetus and corrective imperative for writing American history across the twentieth and into the twenty-first century.

Franklin's *From Slavery to Freedom* is not the first textbook of Black history—for example, Carter G. Woodson's *The Negro in Our History* was in its sixth edition in 1932, and Benjamin Brawley's *A Short History of the American Negro* was also in classroom use in the early 1930s. But *From Slavery to Freedom*—in print since 1947—is the perennial text in the canon of the long Black studies movement. With Franklin's *Land of the Free*, we better understand the stakes of telling history and what can happen when a Black scholar dares to step outside of strictly "Negro" subject matter and recalibrate, in this instance, American history.

Franklin wrote *Land of the Free* in 1966 with two other historians, John W. Caughey of UCLA and Ernest R. May of Harvard. They submitted it for adoption as the sole eighth-grade history textbook in the state of California. In 1962 the state had mandated that history be taught more inclusively and, in 1964, that textbooks must provide a "correct portrayal" of African Americans and "other ethnic groups."[19] *Land of the Free*, if adopted, would be used by approximately 450,000 eighth-grade pupils each year.

When the manuscript was submitted to a panel of state historians for review, it immediately became the target of a right-wing book-banning campaign. The book was criticized as being "slanted in the direction of civil rights… with high praise for militant groups and condemnation for the great majority" and designed to both "build up a segment of the country at the expense of the rest of the country" and "instill a guilt complex" on white students.[20] Critics complained that, if African Americans were to be discussed, athletic heroes like Jackie Robinson were acceptable—but not intellectuals such as Du Bois.[21]

A well-funded group called the *Land of the Free* Committee made a twenty-two-minute filmstrip called *Education or Indoctrination?* and used an image of Franklin's face with *The Communist Manifesto* read out as a voice-over afterward. The committee said the book "destroys pride in America's past, develops a guilt complex, mocks American justice, indoctrinates toward communism, is hostile to religious concepts, overemphasizes Negro participation in American history, projects negative thought models, criticizes business and free enterprise, plays politics, foments class hatred, slants and distorts facts, [and] promotes propaganda and poppycock."[22]

Amy Sherald
What's precious inside of him does not care to be known by the mind in ways that diminish its presence (All American), 2017

Ultimately the book itself prevailed. It was modified without evisceration and resubmitted, then finally declared acceptable and adopted for mandatory use in California's eighth-grade classrooms. Nonetheless, many California radio shows for months after continued to devote hours of talk to the topic, the Pasadena filmstrip continued to be shown and debated (without acknowledgment of changes that had been made to the book), and some local school boards continued to resist using the textbook.

Most threatening in *Land of the Free* was not the narrative of the contributions of people of color but rather African American studies' sharpest tool: the critical consciousness that allows us to question the dominance of one social group over another and solely triumphal versions of any text or history. Is the American central narrative of upward mobility and the power of positive thinking much more than a shroud for a frank assessment of the past and its ongoing unresolved inequities? We see this very issue playing out now with the deliberate distortions and manufactured fear surrounding critical race theory, the school of thought and systemic thinking that began in the legal academy with scholars Derrick Bell, Kimberlé Crenshaw, and Richard Delgado. These questions and methodologies were also developed by culture scholars and historians in African American studies. Critical race theory provides tools helpful for understanding that race is a social category and not a biological fact and that racism is best understood systemically rather than instance by instance.

I want to return to the legacy of John Hope Franklin and the contributions of his work in the academy to the larger racial conversation. The latest editions of Franklin's *From Slavery to Freedom* were prepared by historian and former chair of the African American Studies Department at Harvard Evelyn Brooks Higginbotham, who completed the work at Franklin's request before he died. The book came out in 2009 with the first African American president, Barack Obama, on the cover. In this image Obama, depicted in color, faces a black-and-white photograph of the Negro in bondage, visually marking the distance "from slavery to freedom." The American flag is the background, its symbolic glory and possibility restored. The scholar—Dr. Franklin—who researched part of the book from behind a screen erected to segregate Black and white researchers from each other at the Library of Congress has moved from margin to center. The triumphal version of American history Franklin was chided for eschewing when he told the truth about American history in *Land of the Free* now dominates. African American history has been visually moved to the center, in the person of the first Black president.

It is African American studies as a discipline that teaches me to resist simply cheering this cover, which might suggest that the first Black president is the end point of a history. Certainly we know that there is no triumphal end; the Trump presidency made that once again piercingly clear to us. So I take interest in the fact that Obama's back is turned in the chosen image and his face cannot be seen. We are not, as viewers, given the satisfaction of smiling back at a smiling Obama or the populace he addresses in the picture. The crowd's gaze is skeptical, direct. The historical Negro will not be charmed nor cheered by the triumphal present. Attempting to see things as they really are with the unflinching critical eye is, at the end of the day, the way Black people have strategized and survived. The will to the triumphal is understandable in all peoples who have suffered more than their share of oppressions. But the lesson of African American studies is that the call to the triumphal is a siren song. I hope that the ways in which the humanities move along the racial conversation in this country—thorny, difficult, unsettled—will help us think in terms of process rather than finish line and leave us ever more open to the complexities that the humanities and the arts can reveal to us. As much as the election of Obama was a moment to celebrate, I don't see it as conclusive but rather as one more step forward along a very long road. Even symbolic freedom is, in part, unknowable.

In Tony Kushner's theater masterpiece *Angels in America*, the Black nurse Belize pithily describes some of our national ironies. "The white cracker who wrote the National Anthem knew what he was doing. He set the word 'free' to a note so high nobody can reach it."[23] So many continue to fight for universal freedom. The historians and artists envision it. The advocates and protesters put their bodies on the line for it. But we aren't there yet.

"cemetery for the illustrious negro dead"

Dixwell Avenue in New Haven is an iconic artery through the city leading to or from Yale University, where it dead-ends or begins, depending on how you look at it. The avenue was once the historic bustling corridor of Black New Haven, with a string of jazz venues such as the Recorder Club, the Golden Gate, the Playback Club, and the Monterey Cafe where Louis Armstrong, Ella Fitzgerald, Duke Ellington, Billie Holiday, Charlie Parker, Nat King Cole, John Coltrane, and other greats played. Organizations like the Q House were an anchor for Black community growth and empowerment. On Dixwell Avenue, Malcolm X spoke at the dedication of the city's first Black mosque in 1961, and again in 1962 when Black people were activating as "urban renewal" began to push them out of their homes.[24] My son recently lived exactly at that juncture, on the first block of Dixwell Avenue, in the shadow of the trippy neo-Gothic nine-story marvel that is Yale's Payne Whitney Gymnasium. Every time I would drive to visit him, I'd enter and exit via Dixwell.

New Haven is a demographically diverse city by many measures. It is roughly one-third Black, one-third white, and one-third Latinx, with a small Asian population. It is also an immigrant city: about one in six residents are born outside of the United States, and since 1990, the number of immigrant residents in Greater New Haven (a broader set of municipalities centered around the city of New Haven) has doubled. New Haven is a smallish city that is made up of all that America is, but class and racial division is stark.[25] Yale University is the biggest employer in the state of Connecticut. The average per capita income of a New Havener is $26,429, and almost a third of the residents live in poverty. Compare that to Greenwich in the same state, where the per capita income is $101,619 and 6 percent of the population lives in poverty.[26]

On a recent trip to New Haven, I drove as customary down Dixwell and came into abruptly halting traffic. I soon saw that hundreds of people were clustered outside and pouring into a Black church among so many on Dixwell. It was an arresting tableau because most of the crowd

Frank Stewart
St. Louis Cemetery II, 1980

were wearing bright-goldenrod hoodies over or instead of formal funeral clothes. As I inched by, I saw that on the front of those hoodies was a picture of a smiling young Black man, fifteen or sixteen by my guess. That young man was the reason they were gathered. He was the boy who had died.

Black communities are full of people wearing T-shirts and hoodies with the faces of young Black people on them whom their communities mourn and remember. I do not know more about this boy, or this story, or how he died. But this is one way Black people live, die, and are mourned in New Haven. History is marked by what was there and is no longer, and it is kept by the ways we remember. We honor our beloved, who all too often live abbreviated lives and die for reasons related to race, by calling their names and wearing their faces on our bodies.

In literal cemeteries bodies are buried and the places carry the memory of the ritual farewells that have occurred there, where we weep and hear the sound of shovels breaking dirt in four seasons. Then we mark the ground with headstones to make places to return to. Over the years, cemeteries themselves tell stories and become history.

Cemeteries are planned spaces and community spaces.

I think of the carefully tended Confederate cemetery I visited in Selma, Alabama, where Confederate general and first Grand Wizard of the Ku Klux Klan Nathan Bedford Forrest was defeated at the Battle of Selma, though many have cast him as the heroic Defender of Selma. I think of other places I have seen, Jewish cemeteries in Germany and the Hutu and Tutsi mass burial space under the genocide memorial in Rwanda. I think of all the potter's fields—"a public burial place for paupers, unknown persons, and criminals," per the dictionary. I think of the African Burial Ground National Monument in New York City. Who lies there? Who has been remembered and forgotten?

In October 1991 the African burial ground was discovered in Lower Manhattan just as an apartment complex was about to be erected. The bulldozers and cranes halted when archaeologists and anthropologists finally were granted a hearing to discuss what they had long known: approximately fifteen thousand Africans had lived in community on that site from the 1630s to 1795, some enslaved and some free. The ruin told stories of how they organized, moved, worked, and recreated. Some families were found buried together, their skeletons touching. There was evidence of labor, ingenuity, survival, struggle, kinship, and love. We know about their hats and their boots and their dresses and their cooking pots. Who are their descendants and where are they now? What do they know about these people they came from, who lived there? But for the advocacy of the scholars—but for knowledge, but for engaged history, but for Black studies, but for courage and persistence in the face of capitalist expansion—the graves would have been built over, and not until those buildings one day crumbled as most buildings eventually crumble, if you take the very long view, might anyone have known that an entire small civilization was there. The teeth tell the story of malnutrition and what people ate. The bones tell the story of people being beaten in the course of doing their work, which is to say, they were enslaved. The imprint of hair long since vanished tells us how people attended to their grooming, and cowrie shells tell us how they adorned themselves. What did they think was beautiful? How did they think they were beautiful? I believe human beings never stop longing for freedom; what did these people believe possessed the power to help them transcend their condition?

On the side of the road on American highways, it is not uncommon to see bunches of plastic flowers, home-fashioned wooden crosses, and ribbons around trees that tell us someone lost their life there in a car accident. We drive past but take note: a person lived and was sufficiently loved that someone else made a memorial that not only carries memory but also performs the act of admonishing road travelers that people die regularly in car accidents. Perhaps we slow down. Perhaps we mouth a prayer. We keep driving without having learned where they lived or how they lived in society but how they individually died, suddenly, out of community context.

In Prairie View, Texas, there is a roadside memorial to Sandra Bland, the Black woman who filmed her own arrest without cause and died mysteriously in her jail cell hours later. It is off the road so people can pull over, contemplate, and perhaps leave their own tribute. It is a memorial not only to Bland but to police overreach, the violence with which Bland was handled, her fragility, and what we may never know about what happened to her in the jail cell—jailed for a traffic stop—and how she died.

We were here. We walked this earth, we lived in community, we built this city, we tilled this land, we colored and cultured this place. We were unceremoniously taken and so we receremonialize. We ritualize, because we were

Kerry James Marshall
Souvenir II, 1997

unceremoniously taken, because we were owned and *things* like tractors or threshers or sacks of potatoes. Our children were thought to be machines, put to work from when they were very small. Some as young as four or five pulled ropes and chains continuously to operate large, heavy, often elaborately decorated ceiling fans called punkahs, to create a breeze for the plantation guests while they dined and shoo insects from them and their meals, or to cool them while they rested. Other enslaved small children spent the days in tiny stone structures from which they watched the cane, given the charge of running to tell if the valuable crop was set afire. That for the slave was childhood.

People thought to be property or machines or sex dolls died and then Black people figured out a way to remember and memorialize them in death, to animate and humanize them. No wonder then the soul, how we existed and sustained across the by-and-by, was such an important Black belief.

So we memorialized with songs that preserve and pass on indelibly powerful phrases like *wade in the water*: we crossed people over, and then, decades and centuries later, we made art like revelations to enact that crossing over. Alvin Ailey choreographed "Revelations" to those songs and from those rituals he remembered from his Texas childhood—songs sung by people whose many elders were themselves enslaved—and the dance itself became the memorial, marking passage of the "many thousands gone" and how they lived and how they died but were at least properly taken to a place imagined beautiful, the eternal, the by-and-by.

Sometimes we forget that remembering people, and making their work and legacy available, indelible, and strong, is hard work. The scholars, teachers, artists, meaning-makers, family storytellers, work against forgetting. Despite her genius and acclaim, the writer Zora Neale Hurston— novelist, anthropologist, folklorist, theorist, journalist, playwright, and one of the great American writers of the twentieth century—died in a state of penury and was buried in an unmarked grave in a Florida field. Her great, gorgeous Black woman's bildungsroman *Their Eyes Were Watching God* is widely read and taught, thanks largely to the work of Black feminist writers and literary scholars. She is remembered not simply because she was a brilliant writer—that was insufficient, and genius is neglected every day. She is remembered because people did the work of remembering her.

In "Looking for Zora," Alice Walker writes about her pilgrimage to Florida to find Hurston's then-unmarked grave. In that essay Walker writes about walking through waist-high grass in a snaky field, calling Zora's name and looking for the grave. I want to isolate that moment: calling out her name. Black people speak to the dead matter-of-factly across the moat that separates us from them. We speak to the dead with the certainty that if we do it long enough, they will answer. We speak to the dead in so many different ways because we know they left too soon, because we need their navigation, because we need to remember against the force of society's undervaluing us and throwing us away. We speak to the dead because we understand there is but a porous scrim between life and death.

Walker describes her search:

> "Zora!" I yell, as loud as I can (causing Rosalee to jump). "Are you out here?"
>
> "If she is, I sho hope she don't answer you. If she do, I'm gone."
>
> "Zora!" I call again. "I'm here. Are you?"
>
> "If she is," grumbles Rosalee, "I hope she'll keep it to herself."

"Zora!" Then I start fussing with her. "I hope you don't think I'm going to stand out here all day, with these snakes watching me and these ants having a field day. In fact, I'm going to call you just one or two more times."

Walker continues, "There are times—and finding Zora Hurston's grave was one of them—when normal responses of grief, horror, and so on do not make sense because they bear no real relation to the depth of the emotion one feels. It was impossible for me to cry when I saw the field full of weeds where Zora is." Eventually she found the weedy grave and had it marked with a headstone that reads, "Zora Neale Hurston: 'A Genius of the South.'"[27]

Hurston also left herself for us to find in letters. Letter writing is one of her underestimated art forms, where we sometimes see her as a visionary Black political philosopher clearly offering a radical epistemology for Black freedom that characterized much of what she said, did, and wrote. The letters show many facets of her voice: brilliant, irreverent, persuasive, flirtatious, insightful, profound, and wholly original.

Hurston did not always get on with so-called Negro

establishment figures. Her vitality and forthrightness were sometimes taken as unbecoming of the race. She had a keen pretension-meter and at one point called Du Bois a "goateed, egotistic, wishy-washy...haughty aristocrat."[28] But that didn't stop her from writing him a letter in 1945 with a prophetic idea: "As Dean of American Negro Artists," she wrote, "...[w]hy do you not propose a cemetery for the illustrious Negro dead? Something like Pere la Chaise in Paris." She names the many Black achievers who might lie in it, and envisions it on lush Florida terrain, suggesting that "Negro sculptors and painters decorate it with scenes from our own literature and life. Mythology and all." She concludes her argument, "Let no Negro celebrity, no matter what financial condition they might be in at death, lie in inconspicuous forgetfulness," haunting words when you think about her own demise fifteen years after.[29] Du Bois replied bureaucratically and without much enthusiasm, and the idea did not take root.[30]

Hurston profoundly understood the expendability of Black life. She had a historian's sense of the need to preserve. She knew memorials mattered, and she knew it was up to Black people to make the memorials and tell the stories themselves. I think of libraries and archives and poems and art and other forms of cultural expression in some way as "cemeter[ies] for the illustrious Negro dead," places where Hughes and Hurston and Wright converse with each other and are audible to those who go and pay attention.

Hurston imagined something else that is still sometimes hard to imagine: Negro rest, the much-deserved proper resting place after lives of service and struggle. Percy Sutton had to fight to get Malcolm X interred—when he was assassinated in 1965, no New York cemetery would have him, until Sutton intervened and secured him a spot in Westchester County at Ferncliff Cemetery, where James Baldwin, Paul Robeson, John Lennon, Béla Bartók, Joan Crawford, Moms Mabley, Thelonious Monk, Jerome Kern, and Ed Sullivan also lie. My paternal grandparents, Clifford Leopold Alexander Sr. and Edith McAllister Alexander, lie there too. Libraries and archives are also resting places, not for bones but for documents that can speak across the years and tell our stories.

I began with a visit back to New Haven, to see my younger son. I lived in New Haven for longer than I have ever lived anywhere else. I went to college there, returned after years working, studying, and teaching in Washington, Boston, Philadelphia, and Chicago, and raised my children there from birth to high school before moving to New York. New Haven is a town that holds me tight.

There once was a cobalt-blue house that I passed every day while taking my first son to and from day care. It sat in the middle of the Newhallville community—which is bounded on one side by Dixwell Avenue—with a broad clearing of lot space around it. I never saw people as we drove by. I always wondered who lived there, who chose to paint it that color, did they call upon ancestral understanding of the power of that blue to keep evil spirits away, to protect the occupants of the house, the blue the same blue as an evil eye, or a Mexican doorway, or a Greek doorway, or an African doorway? Why did someone paint that house that blue? It would have been untoward to knock on the door. Who lived in that house?

And one day I drove by, and there was but a vacant lot. The house was entirely gone. It had been razed. There was no trace. I pulled the car over and walked to the lot to look for a board or shingle, a splinter, even, of the blue in the rubble in that lot. I could not find it. But I know the blue was there. Any time I pass that lot—twenty years later in this dear city, still vacant—I think of that house, and I think of the things I did not know about the people who lived in it. I cannot imagine that the power of that color did not speak to others in the neighborhood that I daily passed through.

The not-there cobalt house now feels like a memorial to people who rarely had a fair chance. They were eviscerated from their community when the university and the town wanted to make a model community for white people, and they were never reresourced or relocated. The rest of the neighborhood was left to the Black folks who were still there, but with a chunk of their community scooped out and the clear knowledge that no one but themselves was going to invest in their thriving, in the shadow of one of the wealthiest universities in the world. And yet: the cobalt house, its power and juju, its beauty, its memory.

The artist-architect Amanda Williams painted a series of abandoned and condemned houses in a neighborhood on the South Side of Chicago in the iconic colors of products overconsumed in the food desert: Flamin' Hot Cheetos orange, Newport cigarettes teal, Crown Royal whiskey bag purple. The colors blazed with familiarity. The community had the opportunity to look at the colors of the junk that is marketed and sold to them, and then when the houses were finally destroyed, watch them disappear. The vacancy in their place was perhaps an absence, perhaps a possibility. Their absence changed nothing, explicitly. But all that powerful culture in the face of the violence that affects us, and the vernacular expression of spirits that will not be broken, must be noted.

I wonder, do I really believe that cultural expression can somehow shape a world where our children are safer?

PART II

Dawoud Bey
Martina and Rhonda, Chicago, IL, 1993

the trayvon generation

This one was shot in his grandmother's yard. This one was carrying a bag of Skittles. This one was playing with a toy gun in front of a gazebo. Black girl in bright bikini. Black boy holding cell phone. This one danced like a marionette as he was shot down in a Chicago intersection. The words, the names: *Trayvon, Laquan, bikini, gazebo, loosies, Skittles, two seconds, I can't breathe, traffic stop, dashboard cam, sixteen times.* His dead body lay in the street in the August heat for four hours.

He was jogging, was hunted down, cornered by a pickup truck, and shot three times. One of the men who murdered him leaned over his dead body and was heard to say, "Fucking nigger."

I can't breathe, again. Nine minutes and twenty-nine seconds of a knee and full weight on his neck. "I can't breathe" and, then, "Mama!" George Floyd cried. George Floyd cried, "Mama...I'm through!"

His mother had been dead for two years when George Floyd called out for her as he was being lynched. Lynching is defined as a killing committed by a mob. I call the four police officers who arrested him a mob.

The kids got shot and the grown-ups got shot. Which is to say, the kids watched their peers shot down and their parents' generation get gunned down and beat down and terrorized as well. The agglomerating spectacle continues. Here are a few we know less well: Danny Ray Thomas. Johnnie Jermaine Rush. Nania Cain. Dejuan Hall. Atatiana Jefferson. Demetrius Bryan Hollins. Jacqueline Craig and her children. And then the iconic: Alton Sterling. Eric Garner. Sandra Bland. Walter Scott. Breonna Taylor. Philando Castile.

Sandra Bland filmed the prelude to her death. The policeman thrust a stun gun in her face and said, "I will light you *up*."

I call the young people who grew up in the past twenty-five years the Trayvon Generation. They always knew these stories. These stories formed their worldview. These stories helped instruct young African Americans about their embodiment and their vulnerability. The stories were primers in fear and futility. The stories were the ground soil of their rage. The stories instructed them that anti-Black hatred and violence were never far.

They watched these violations up close and on their cell phones, so many times over. They watched them in near-real time. They watched them crisscrossed and concentrated. They watched them on the school bus. They watched them under the covers at night. They watched them often outside of the presence of adults who loved them and were charged with keeping them safe in body and soul.

This is the generation of my sons, now twenty-three and twenty-two years old, and their friends who are also children to me, and the university students I have taught and mentored and loved. And this is also the generation of Darnella Frazier, the seventeen-year-old Minneapolis girl who came upon George Floyd's murder in progress while on an everyday run to the corner store on May 25, filmed it on her phone, and posted it to her Facebook page at 1:46 a.m., with the caption "They killed him right in front of cup foods over south on 38th and Chicago!! No type of sympathy </3 </3 #POLICEBRUTALITY." When

insideMPD.com (in an article that is no longer up) wrote, "Man Dies after Medical Incident during Police Interaction," Frazier posted at 3:10 a.m., "Medical incident??? Watch outtt they killed him and the proof is clearlyyyy there!!"

Darnella Frazier, seventeen years old, witnessing a murder in close proximity, making a record that would have worldwide impact, returned the following day to the scene of the crime. She possessed the language to say, precisely, through tears, "It's so traumatizing."

In Toni Morrison's *Sula*, which is set across the bleak black stretch of Ohio after the First World War, the character Hannah plaintively asks her mother, Eva Peace, "Mamma, did you ever love us?" To paraphrase Eva Peace's reply: *Love you? Love you? I kept you alive.*[31]

I believed I could keep my sons alive by loving them, believed in the magical powers of complete adoration and a love ethic that would permeate their lives. My love was armor when they were small. My love was armor when their father died of a heart attack when they were twelve and thirteen. "They think Black men only die when they get shot," my older son said in the aftermath. My love was armor when that same year our community's block watch sent emails warning residents about "two Black kids on bikes" and praising neighbors who had called the police on them. My love for my children said, *Move*. My love said, *Follow your sons* when they ran into the dark streets of New York to join protesters after Eric Garner's killer was acquitted. When my sons were in high school and pictures of Philando Castile were on the front page of the *Times*, I wanted to burn all the newspapers so they would not see the gun coming in the window, the blood on Castile's T-shirt, the terror in his partner's face, and the eyes of his witnessing baby girl. But I was too late, too late generationally, because they were not looking at the newspaper; they were looking at their phones, where the image was a house of mirrors straight to hell.

My love was both rational and fantastical. Can I protect my sons from being demonized? Can I keep them from moving free? But they must be able to move as free as wind! If I listen to their fears, will I comfort them? If I share my fears, will I frighten them? Will racism and fear disable them? If we ignore it all, will it go away? Will dealing with race fill their minds like stones and block them from thinking of a million other things? Let's be clear about what motherhood is. A being comes onto this earth and you are charged with keeping it alive. It dies if you do

Elizabeth Catlett
The Torture of Mothers, 1970

not tend it. It is as simple as that. No matter how intellectual and multicolored motherhood becomes as children grow older, the part that says, *My purpose on earth is to keep you alive* has never totally dissipated. Magical thinking on all sides.

I want my children—all of them—to thrive, to be fully alive. How do we measure what that means? What does it mean for our young people to be "black alive and looking back at you," as June Jordan puts it in her poem "Who Look at Me"?[32] How to access the sources of strength that transcend this American nightmare of racism and racist violence? What does it mean to be a lucky mother, when so many of my sisters have had their children taken from them by this hatred? The painter Titus Kaphar's recent *Time* magazine cover portrays a Black mother cradling what should be her child across the middle of her body, but the child is literally cut out of the canvas and cut out of the mother, leaving a gaping wound for an unending grief that has made a sisterhood of countless Black women for generations.

My sons were both a little shy outside of our home when they were growing up. They were quiet and observant, like their father, who had come to this country as a refugee from

Eritrea: African observant, immigrant observant, missing nothing. I've watched them over the years with their friends, doing dances now outmoded with names I persist in loving—Nae Nae, Hit Dem Folks—and talking about things I didn't teach them and reading books I haven't read and taking positions I don't necessarily hold, and I marvel. They are grown young men. With their friends, they talk about the pressure to succeed, to have a strong public face, to excel. They talk their big talk, they talk their hilarity, and they talk their fear. When I am with them, I truly believe the kids are all right and will save us.

But I worry about this generation of young Black people and depression. I have a keen eye—what Gwendolyn Brooks called "gobbling mother-eye"—for these young people, sons and friends and students whom I love and encourage and welcome into my home, keep in touch with and check in on.[33] *How are you, how are you, how are you. How are you, baby, how are you.* I am interested in the vision of television shows like *Atlanta* and *Insecure*, about which I have been asking every young person who will listen, "Don't you think they're about low-grade, undiagnosed depression and not Black hipster ennui?" Why, in fact, did Earn drop out of Princeton? Why does Van get high before a drug test? Why does Issa keep blowing up her life? This season, *Insecure* deals directly with the question of young Black people and mental-health issues: Molly is in and out of therapy, and we learn that Nathan, aka LyftBae, who was ghosting Issa, has been dealing with bipolar disorder. The work of the creative icon of their generation often brings me to the question: Why is Kendrick so sad? He has been frank about his depression and suicidal thoughts. It isn't just the specter of race-based violence and death that hangs over these young people. It's that compounded with the constant display of inequity that has most recently been laid bare in the COVID-19 pandemic, with racial health disparities that are shocking even to those of us inured to our disproportionate suffering.

Black creativity emerges from long lines of innovative responses to the death and violence that plague our communities. "Not a house in the country ain't packed to its rafters with some dead Negro's grief," Toni Morrison wrote in *Beloved*, and I am interested in creative emergences from that ineluctable fact.[34]

There are so many visual artists responding to this changing same: Henry Taylor, Michael Rakowitz, Ja'Tovia Gary, Carrie Mae Weems, lauren woods, Alexandra Bell,

Black Women Artists for Black Lives Matter, Steffani Jemison, Kerry James Marshall, Titus Kaphar. To pause at one work: Dread Scott's *A Man Was Lynched by Police Yesterday*, which he made in the wake of the police shooting of Walter Scott in 2015, echoes the flag reading "A MAN WAS LYNCHED YESTERDAY" that the NAACP flew outside its New York headquarters between 1920 and 1938 to mark the lynchings of Black people in the United States.

I want to turn to three short films that address the Trayvon Generation with particular power: Flying Lotus's *Until the Quiet Comes* (2012); his *Never Catch Me*, featuring Kendrick Lamar (2014); and Lamar's *Alright* (2015).

In *Until the Quiet Comes*, the director, Kahlil Joseph, moves us through Black Los Angeles—Watts, to be specific. In the fiction of the video, a boy stands in an empty swimming pool, pointing his finger as a gun and shooting. The bullet ricochets off the wall of the pool and he drops as it appears to hit him. The boy lies in a wide-arced swath of his blood, a portrait in the empty pool. He is another Black boy down, another body of the traumatized community.

In an eerie twilight, we move into the densely populated Nickerson Gardens, where a young man, played by the dancer Storyboard P, lies dead. Then he rises and begins

Charles White
Banner for Willie J., 1976

a startling dance of resurrection, perhaps coming back to life. The community seems numb, oblivious to his rebirth. That rebirth is brief; he gets into a low-rider car, that LA icon. The car drives off after his final death dance, taking him from this life to the other side. His death is consecrated by his performance, a ritual that the suddenly dead are not afforded. The car becomes a hearse, a space of ritual transport into the next life. But the young man is still gone.

What does it mean to be able to bring together the naturalistic and the visionary, to imagine community as capable of reanimating even its most hopeless and anesthetized members? What does it mean for a presumably murdered Black body to come to life in his community in a dance idiom that is uniquely part of Black culture and youth culture, all of that power channeled into a lifting?

A sibling to Joseph's work is Hiro Murai's video for Flying Lotus's "Never Catch Me." It opens at a funeral for two children, a Black boy and girl, who lie heartbreak-beautiful in their open caskets. Their community grieves inconsolably in the church. The scene is one of profound mourning.

And then the children open their eyes and climb out of their caskets. They dance explosively in front of the pulpit before running down the aisle and out of the church. The mourners cannot see this resurrection, for it is a fantasia. The kids dance another dance of Black LA, the force of Black bodily creativity, that expressive life source born of violence and violation that have upturned the world for generations. The resurrected babies dance with a pumping force. But the community's grief is unmitigated, because, once again, this is a dreamscape. The children spring out into the light and climb into a car—no, it is a hearse—and, smiling with the joy of mischievous escapees, drive away. Kids are not allowed to drive; kids are not allowed to die.

What does it mean for a Black boy to fly, to dream of flying and transcending? To imagine his vincible body all-powerful, a body that in this society is so often consumed as a moneymaker and an object of perverse desire, perceived to have superhuman and thus threatening powers? In the video for Kendrick Lamar's "Alright," directed by Colin Tilley, Lamar flies through the California city streets, above sidewalks and empty lots, alongside wire fences.

"Alright" has been the anthem of many protests against racism and police violence and unjust treatment. Lamar embodies the energy and the message of the resonant phrase *Black Lives Matter*, which Patrisse Cullors, Alicia

Garza, and Opal Tometi catapulted into circulation when, in 2013, they founded the movement. The phrase was apt then and now. Its coinage feels both ancestral in its knowledge and prophetic in its ongoing necessity. I know now with certainty that there will never be a moment when we will not need to say it, not in my lifetime, and not in the lifetime of the Trayvon Generation.

The young Black man flying in Lamar's video is joyful and defiant, rising above the streets that might claim him, his body liberated and autonomous. At the end of the video, a police officer raises a finger to the young man in the sky and mimes pulling a trigger. The wounded young man falls, slowly—another brother down—and lands. The gun was a finger; the flying young man appears safe. He does not get up. But in the final image of this dream he opens his eyes and smiles. For a moment, he has not been killed.

Black celebration is a village practice that has brought us together in protest and ecstasy around the globe and across time. Community is a mighty life force for self-care and survival. But it does not protect against murder. Dance itself will not free us. We continue to struggle against hatred and violence. I believe that this generation is more vulnerable, and more traumatized, than the last. I think of Frederick Douglass's words upon hearing slaves singing their sorrow songs in the fields. He laid waste to the nascent myth of the happy darky: "Slaves sing most when they are most unhappy."[35] Our dancing is our pleasure, but perhaps it is also our sorrow song.

My sons love to dance. I have raised them to young adulthood. They are beautiful. They are funny. They are strong. They are fascinating. They are kind. They are joyful in friendship and community. They are righteous and smart in their politics. They are learning. They are loving. They are mighty and alive.

I recall many sweaty summer parties with family friends where the grown-ups regularly acted up on the dance floor and the kids deejayed to see how quickly they could make their old-school parents and play-uncles and -aunties holler, "Aaaaayyyy! That's my jam!" They watched us with deep amusement. But they would dance too. One of the aunties glimpsed my sons around the corner in the next room and said, "Oh my God, they can dance! They've been holding out on us, acting all shy!"

When I told a sister-friend that my older son, during his freshman year in college, was often the one controlling the aux cord, dancing and dancing and dancing, she said, "Remember, people dance when they are joyful."

Yes, I am saying I measure my success as a mother of Black boys in part by the fact that I have sons who love to dance, who dance in community, who dance till their powerful bodies sweat, who dance and laugh, who dance and shout. Who are able—in the midst of their studying and organizing, their fear, their rage, their protesting, their vulnerability, their missteps and triumphs, their knowledge that they must fight the hydra-headed monster of racism and racial violence that we were not able to cauterize—to find the joy and the power of communal self-expression.

This is not a celebration, nor is it an elegy.

We are no longer enslaved. Langston Hughes wrote that we must stand atop the racial mountain, "free within ourselves," and I pray that those words have meaning for our young people.[36] But our freedom must be seized and reasserted every day.

People dance to say, *I am alive and in my body.*

I am black alive and looking back at you.

PART III

Chandra McCormick

Daddy'O, The Oldest Inmate in Angola State Penitentiary, 2004

"we dress our ideas in clothes to make the abstract visible"

I am looking at a photograph called *Daddy'O, The Oldest Inmate in Angola State Penitentiary*. A Black man in prison-issue jeans and shirt leans against a tree, his right hand across his heart and his left resting at an angle on his thigh. He looks both calm and distressed, peaceful and haunted. He was seventy-five when the photo was taken by Chandra McCormick, a photographer from New Orleans who along with her husband Keith Calhoun has chronicled Angola prison and its inmates and visitors for many years. They took one iconic photograph of a guard on a horse, surveying the incarcerated men picking cotton in the field, and many other pictures that haunt. Daddy'O is the one I return to: his knitted brow, his hand on his heart, the experiences on his face, the stories behind his eyes, and all that they have seen. He served fifteen years in Angola and was then released, spent a few weeks on the outside, and was put in again, where he served time until he died there.[37]

The Louisiana State Penitentiary, known as Angola, sits outside of New Orleans on land the size of the island of Manhattan. It looks today like the plantation it was, with Black men picking cotton, or okra, while white correctional officers ride on horseback to oversee their work. All that is missing in the tableau is the whip. It is both emblem and manifestation of the crisis of mass incarceration in this country and its disproportionate impact on people of color, inside and outside the prisons and the neighborhoods and communities they draw from. Incarcerated people are too often forgotten, sent away and out of sight, far from people who love them, with tremendous obstacles to strong relationships.

The extraordinary documentary *Time*, by Garrett Bradley, follows the Rob and Sibil Fox Richardson family through the years of their teenaged courtship, the birth of six sons, and Rob's robbery conviction, sixty-year sentence, incarceration at Angola, and eventual release. The title is apt: the film, which is in large part compiled of home video that Fox recorded and preserved, gives a strange and surreal sense of how time spools both quickly and interminably across the family-defining years of Rob's incarceration. Fox will not let her family unravel, and holding Rob both in the present and in the light of memory when he is locked away is her achievement and what the film bears witness to and allows viewers to see and share.

Angola houses the largest population of lifers on planet Earth, and by many estimates, at least 90 percent of those incarcerated will die there.[38] I planned a trip there with a group of colleagues doing philanthropic work in New Orleans because to understand the City of New Orleans we needed to include and see this place that cages upwards of six thousand people, most of whom hail from Orleans or Jefferson Parish. Here or not here, they are here.

We were interested in the *Angolite*, the George Polk Award–winning prison newsmagazine, and the radio station, and the famous hospice. I wanted to learn more about the many musicians who served significant time there: Lead Belly, two of the Neville Brothers, James Booker. Musicologists John and Alan Lomax believed that because of the intense isolation and privation at prisons like Angola and Mississippi's Parchman Farm, also a former plantation, certain powerful forms of Black music developed and were sustained within their walls.

The second-oldest Neville brother, Charles, served five years in Angola in the early 1960s for possession of two marijuana joints. When he got out, he sang and recorded with his brothers songs like "Angola Bound" that were created inside the prison. Angola has drawn attention from many other artists. Deborah Luster is a white photographer who, after the murder of her mother, sought to explore and reconcile her feelings by photographing a wide range of people in Angola. She published it in the book *One Big Self: Prisoners of Louisiana*, which she made with the late poet C. D. Wright.[39]

The prisoners brought what they could to their portrait sessions—what they owned, what they could borrow—to shape the message they wanted to send out through the image. Luster creates these portraits as tintypes, a beautiful and anachronistic form that creates a single image. The effect is one of suspended time. On the reverse, Luster engraves names, birthdates, birthplaces, nicknames, how many children they might have, hobbies, interests, aspirations, and dreams. She also includes their Department of Corrections ID numbers, where they are incarcerated, the length of sentence, their assigned jobs within the prison system—such as chair factory, work field, or metal fab.

Luster then gave those photographed their portraits, a moment of ownership over their own image and a meaningful way to connect with loved ones on the outside.

"I returned twenty-five thousand prints to inmates," Luster says. "They made themselves so vulnerable for me, and it's not often that you have an encounter like that. I know a lot of it was that they were actually posing for the people that they loved—their husbands, their wives, their children." She continues,

> There was a woman who asked to be photographed. She said, "I've been here fifteen years. I'm down for ninety-nine years. I have nineteen children. My children haven't spoken to me since I came to prison. Perhaps if I had some photographs I could send them, it would soften their hearts to me." A few months later, she said, "Four of my children came to visit me. The baby came and he's now nineteen. He was five years old when I came to prison."[40]

The photographs capture the sitters with the formality of remembrance, some of the millions of not-dead

Deborah Luster

E. C. P. P. F.
Transylvania, Louisiana

Eddie M. "Fat" CoCo
d.o.b. 6·30·79
p.o.b. New Orleans
Sentence · 6 years
Children · 2 boys
Future plans · Be success/
                        Lawyer

69

photo 3·8·02

CA/p

Eddie M. "Fat" Coco Jr., Transylvania, Louisiana, March 8, 2002 separated from society. If we forget them, we will not understand who, in total, we are.

Picking cotton is the first rotation men do when they are brought into Angola, for which they earn between four and forty cents an hour.[41] The prisoners are almost exclusively Black. The guards are almost exclusively white. I read on the wall in the small entry museum that in 1835 Black women prisoners were there because they resisted the conditions of slavery.

Some of those men—not men, those fifteen-year-olds—were not in prison for life without parole because of rape or premeditated murder but some for "reckless eyeballing."

"Reckless eyeballing" is a concept most infamous for its use by pre–civil rights courts to punish and imprison Black men for looking at white women.[42] However, it is still used for any form of gaze deemed "aggressive" or "inappropriate," especially when a Black person looks a white person with power directly in the eye. Black incarcerated men are frequently thrown into solitary confinement for making direct eye contact with their white guards.[43]

There is a membership golf course on the property for people outside the prison. From the restaurant and the golf course you can view the infamous Camp J, where men are kept in solitary confinement. I asked the warden if we might drive by Camp J, and the warden told us no.

There is entertainment at the prison provided for outsiders, including a famous rodeo.

We did not see the rodeo.

We did not see Camp J.

We did not see the camels that are kept on the property for the nativity scene that is assembled every year on the golf course.

We did visit a writing and meditation group that was called a "compassion group." In the group we heard men speak about meditating, about understanding why people have pain, understanding who they are, learning to be reflective. The sessions last eight weeks and an inmate can attend once in his entire time in the prison, eight weeks in literally a lifetime in the case of most of the men in the room.

One man, perhaps thirty-five, told us he had been sentenced to life when he was fifteen.

The writing group was all Black men. The teacher was a white woman who created a literal, physical circle in which the men talked about themselves and their lives in response to a reading. The stated goal of the group, according to the warden, was "to make the men calm."

At least 90 percent of the men imprisoned there will die there. As a guest, I stood outside the circle, but as I listened I could not help but move in because the human force drew me in and it felt wrong to stand outside. One of the men, who had been in prison since he was a teenager, said, "We dress our ideas in clothes to make the abstract visible." The phrase arrested me. I thought about my own career as a professor and about the thin line that separated some of the young men I have taught from these young men. If any student of mine spoke these words I would have leaned closer, been drawn in by the image, and asked to understand more.

This life is the only life. There is no liberation in the by-and-by.

The warden and I both cried when we left the writing group.

We then asked to see the hospice that has been praised in more than one film. Hospice provides a way to leave this earth with dignity. What does it mean to have a hospice for a population when fifteen-year-olds have been sentenced to life without parole, which is to say to die there?

What does it mean to a middle-aged person condemned while still a teenager to die in prison to have eight weeks out of his entire life in a mindfulness group?

I want to tell you about Herman Wallace. He was convicted of armed robbery and sent to Angola in 1971. Once there he established the Angola chapter of the Black Panther Party with Ronald Ailsworth, Albert Woodfox, and Gerald Bryant after receiving permission from the Panther central office in Oakland. The Angola Panthers organized to improve conditions at the prison, which made them targets of the administration.

In 1972 a white prison guard named Brent Miller was murdered inside Angola. By 1974 Wallace and Woodfox were convicted for the murder, with no physical evidence linking them to the scene of the crime. After the murder Wallace, Woodfox, and Robert King were put in solitary, where they were held for more than forty years—the longest period anyone has been held in solitary confinement in American history—until their release was secured.

Artist jackie sumell learned of Wallace's story in 2001 and shortly thereafter wrote to him, commencing a twelve-year friendship during which they exchanged over three hundred letters and many phone calls. While at Stanford as an MFA student, sumell received the assignment of asking a professor to describe their most exorbitant dream home, in order to study spatial relationships. "I struggled to balance the futility of my assignment—which reinforced the power dynamics of wealth, race, and privilege—with the stark reality of Herman's condition," she wrote in an artist statement later.[44] So she turned to Herman, rather than a Stanford professor, and asked the seemingly simple question:

> What kind of house does a man who has lived
> in a six-foot-by-nine-foot box for almost thirty
> years dream of?

Over the ensuing weeks and months, he imagined and described to her a house meticulously designed, with a black panther on the bottom of the swimming pool, photographs of Black heroes, a bar with martini glasses. It had a library with books about Black liberation and an iconic seventies fur throw across the end of the bed.

She designed and drew the house he visioned, and then made a maquette of it, and then began to create architectural renderings, down to every detail. Through their

jackie sumell
Herman Wallace's Conference Room, 2008

letters and her practice of and faith in the power of what art can do, they activated the power of his imagination and creativity to vision his freedom and future, even when his release was not remotely likely.

While she was working on the house, his conviction was overturned. Herman Wallace was released from prison. He visited with sumell, and his family, and celebrated his freedom.

He died three days later.

sumell finished *Herman's House* as a moveable work of art and has toured it in art spaces around the country. She continues to keep Herman's legacy alive through the *Solitary Gardens* project, where solitary confinement cells are turned into equally sized garden beds. Incarcerated prisoners in solitary confinement design the gardens' plant life and tend to them in collaboration with those on the outside.

It started with a question to a man who lived forty-one years in solitary confinement for a crime he did not commit.

Before I saw Angola prison myself, and walked where the thousands and thousands of human beings whose lives have been affected by it lived, these artists showed me so.

More of us can know because the art sees for us and carries traces of the lives of the human beings who are remembered by their loved ones and whom we cannot turn away from.

What do you picture when you picture your home?

Robert Pruitt
Untitled (Male Celestial Body), 2016

"whether the negro sheds tears"

On April 3, 1905, a researcher named Alvin Borgquist at Clark University in Worcester, Massachusetts, wrote to the preeminent scholar, activist, writer, theorist, and chronicler of race W. E. B. Du Bois at his academic home of Atlanta University. Borgquist wrote:

> *Dear Sir:*
>
> *We are pursuing an investigation here on the subject of crying as an expression of the emotions, and should like very much to learn about its peculiarities among the colored people. We have been referred to you as a person competent to give us information upon the subject. We desire especially to know about the following salient aspects.*
>
> 1. *Whether the negro sheds tears.*
> 2. *If so, under what general conditions—anger, fear, shame, pain, sorrow, etc.*

3. *As regards any peculiarities in vocalization.*
4. *As to what extent crying is controlled either for effect, or on the side of inhibition.*
5. *In regard to its mental and physical effect upon him, whether he may soon recover and feel light and gay, apparently refreshed, or whether it is exhaustive and leaves him weary, sullen, or depressed.*
6. *As to any difference in age or sex in any of these respects.*

Any information on any of these topics will be grate-fully received.

Very sincerely,
Alvin Borgquist
(Clark University, Worcester, Mass.)[45]

Black people were, to this researcher, not understood to do something as fundamentally human as cry. The query was a question: *Does the negro shed tears?*

Think of the first sign that marks human beings as human and alive: a baby's cry at birth. Think of crying and all that it expresses and carries, and crying as a fundamentally involuntary human expression, like laughter.

The researcher wanted to know if Black people cried. Which in essence means, as a query to Du Bois, Do you and your people feel? Are you human?

Almost a hundred years later, the poet Michael S. Harper took up what seems to be the same story in his poem "Deathwatch." He describes his and his wife's intimate and aching loss of a child at birth—a Black son lost—and the intense feelings that ravaged them. Then the poem turns sharply to another version of the Du Bois story:

> This is a dedication
> to our memory
> of three sons—
> two dead, one alive—
> a reminder of a letter
> to DuBois
> from a student
> at Cornell—on behalf
> of his whole history class.
> The class is confronted
> with a question,
> and no one—
> not even the professor—

is sure of the answer:
"Will you please tell us
whether or not it is true
that negroes
are not able to cry?"

Are Black people human. Are Black people human? Do Black people do what people do. Are Black people people. If Black people are not people and do not cry, then they do not experience pain, or grief, or trauma, or shock, or sorrow. If Black people do not experience pain, or grief, or trauma, or shock, or sorrow, are they human? And if they are not human, can their continued violation be justified? Can Black people be harmed if they cannot cry to say so?

Du Bois replied to Borgquist a few days later in a letter that is a list poem unto itself. The first line simply reads, "The negro sheds tears."[46]

We Black people are made mostly of water, blood, and tears. Our black/gold/brown/sienna/blue-black/yellow/ yella/cream/umber/chocolate/sand/wet sand/beige/acorn/ black skin contains those waters. We bleed; we shed oceans of tears. Our waters contain our sorrows.

Almost a year after George Floyd was killed, I watch the

trial of Derek Chauvin, the former police officer who killed him by kneeling on his neck for over nine minutes. Again, as with the video, I want to turn away but I cannot turn away, because I feel I have to witness.

A pulmonologist named Dr. Martin J. Tobin, testifying for the prosecution, takes us quietly and inexorably through a meticulous close read of the video of the killing, noting details such as this: Floyd's boot toe off the ground means half of Chauvin's weight, 86.9 pounds, is being pressed into Floyd's neck. He shows us Floyd fighting for breath with every fiber of his being, illuminating the efforts made with any slightly liberated body part to move to create an airway. When Floyd braces his knuckles on the ground, Dr. Tobin says, "This shows he has used up all his resources and showed he is trying to breathe with his fingers and knuckles."

He tells us the precise second—five minutes and three seconds in—that Floyd has suffered a catastrophic brain injury. The kneeling on the neck continues for long minutes after that. Then Dr. Tobin shows us the exact moment of Floyd's death. "One second he's alive and one second he's no longer. That's the moment that life goes out of his body."[47]

Charles McMillian, a neighborhood elder at sixty-one, weeps on the stand and cannot stop. "I feel helpless. I don't have a mama either. I understand him."[48] George Floyd's brother Philonise cries on the stand when shown a photograph of himself as a child with his older brother, George. He says, "[George] was a big momma's boy. I cry a lot, but George, he loved his mom.... He showed us how to treat our mom, how to respect our mom. He loved her *so* dearly."[49] All the Black men in this trial seem to cry. And the young people say they should have done something to stop it. The young man at the store who was the cashier for Floyd's transaction wishes he hadn't questioned the counterfeit bill. Black people, including unimaginably brave Darnella Frazier, say, *I should have intervened. I should have stopped it.* The young people assume responsibility for the horror they could not prevent.

George Floyd cried for his mother as he died.

I see Black elders cry watching this trial.

As millions waited for the verdict in the Chauvin trial, police killed a sixteen-year-old girl in Columbus, Ohio, Ma'Khia Bryant.

In tears are sorrow. In tears are grief, in tears are anger.

In tears are rage. In tears swallowed are cancer, hypertension, respiratory ailments. In tears swallowed is dis-ease. In tears shed is sometimes no relief on the other side.

Black tears unshed and swallowed every day. And Black tears shed.

"there are black people in the future"

The artist Alisha B. Wormsley made a work of art that first appeared as a billboard over the racially gentrifying East Liberty neighborhood of Pittsburgh. It reads, "THERE ARE BLACK PEOPLE IN THE FUTURE." She has said, "I do not own the sentence" and has encouraged it for anyone's use: "It belongs to anyone. I want people to use it."[50] There have subsequently been "There are Black People in the Future" billboards in Detroit, Chicago, Kansas City, Houston, New York, East St. Louis, and London, and Wormsley has helped raise grant money for artists, writers, thinkers, and activists to use to engage with the phrase and multiply its power and evocation.

To me the billboard is, at first glance, a joyous surprise in the sky. It brings a chuckle because it states what we hope is the obvious: of course there are Black people in the future. There will always be Black people. Black people are the future, we are forever, and—to riff on Gwendolyn Brooks—we "occur" everywhere.[51] And "BLACK PEOPLE" next to "FUTURE" is an act of conjuration; "THERE ARE" is a promise and a declaration.

But could the continuation of Black people be in question? The artwork raises the specter of vulnerability, and our specific impermanence. This mighty entity called Black people—who survived when we were not meant to, who embodied and defined humanity even when we were legally described as three-fifths human and who, through the indignities of discrimination and struggle, created the culture that rocked the world—could we become extinct? Could the violence and the hatred take us down? Remember, wrote Audre Lorde, "we were never meant to survive."[52] Black people today are the product of people who survived, who were not meant to flourish.

Lucille Clifton's poem "won't you celebrate with me" opens what we think is a joyful space of straightforward celebration. But the short poem concludes with what I would call a blues exultation: "that everyday / something has tried to kill me / and has failed."[53] Black flourishing and futurity occur against the odds. But here we are and yes, we did. Contemporary Black people—if we claim our inheritance—carry not only the hopes and dreams of a generation but also the will and ingenuity to survive.

Something tries to kill us every day. It happens again, as it always happens again. This time the name is Daunte Wright, murdered in Minneapolis in the midst of the Chauvin trial. If our televisions are on that day, we see both of these men being killed by police, over and over again. We also, on this same day, watch Afro-Latino Lieutenant Caron Nazario pulled over, yelled at with belligerent language, continue to calmly ask why he is being pulled over and evenly state that he is on active duty in the armed services and serving this country. "What's going on?" Nazario asks, and the police officer replies, "What's going on is you're fixing to ride the lightning, son," then pepper-sprays and Tasers him.[54]

And then there are the children of color around the country killed by police during the Chauvin trial, in complicated stories that raise questions about what young people are living with alongside the tragedy of their deaths. Adam Toledo, thirteen years old. Ma'Khia Bryant, sixteen years old. The names go on and on.

In addition to showing excessive violence and punishment meted out against Black people, including our children, some of these stories raise the question of how quickly anyone can distance themselves from children they are not immediately responsible for. Gwendolyn Brooks, as always, asks of the community, What does it mean to say we are all responsible for our children, even if we cannot fully protect them?

The Boy Died in My Alley

to Running Boy

The Boy died in my alley
without my Having Known.
Policeman said, next morning,
"Apparently died Alone."

"You heard a shot?" Policeman said.
Shots I hear and Shots I hear.
I never see the Dead.

The Shot that killed him yes I heard
as I heard the Thousand shots before;
careening tinnily down the nights
across my years and arteries.

Policeman pounded on my door.
"Who is it?" "POLICE!" Policeman yelled.
"A Boy was dying in your alley.
A Boy is dead, and in your alley.
And have you known this Boy before?"

I have known this Boy before.
I have known this boy before, who
ornaments my alley.
I never saw his face at all.
I never saw his futurefall.
But I have known this Boy.

I have always heard him deal with death.
I have always heard the shout, the volley.
I have closed my heart-ears late and early.
And I have killed him ever.

I joined the Wild and killed him
with knowledgeable unknowing.
I saw where he was going.
I saw him Crossed. And seeing,
I did not take him down.

He cried not only "Father!"

but "Mother!
Sister!
Brother."
The cry climbed up the alley.
It went up to the wind.
It hung upon the heaven
for a long
stretch-strain of Moment.

The red floor of my alley
is a special speech to me.

I have known this boy; we all could be this boy; we must see this boy as our child; we must know one another. We are responsible to and for each other.

In Renée Cox's 1998 photograph *Rajé to the Rescue*, a Black woman superhero flies through time and history in order to show the way to a more liberated future. Foxy in her Afro–Wonder Woman costume, dreadlocks flying, she soars past the Egyptian Sphinx giving a jaunty salute that says, *I got this.* In other of Cox's Rajé photographs, the character is shown escorting Aunt Jemima and Uncle Ben off of their boxes, lifting a taxicab—presumably off of someone trapped beneath—in the middle of Times Square, sitting atop the Statue of Liberty and saluting, campaigning for president of the United States. Rajé allows us to imagine the future and envisions literal Black female might unfettered. If we could change history, if we could be ourselves and not stereotypes, if we could be trusted to govern, if we could stand for the freedom that is promised in the Statue of Liberty but not yet achieved—asks Rajé—the world might be safer, more just, and more exhilarating. Rajé evokes a smile as does the Wormsley billboard—the tonic of survival-laughter—as she goes about her dead-serious mission.

Rajé is in the future. She blazes across an artist-made sky, marking space where we are free. We make freedom within. We call the ancestors and elders to help us build it. How do Black artists imagine a freedom and articulate freedom when its contours and testing grounds change with each generation? How do they see it when we have not fully lived it? What power sources can we call on in our tradition?

My father is a very free Black man, and once you have been inculcated with that worldview there is no acceptable alternative. Even if we understand the way racism

Renée Cox
Chillin' with Liberty, 1998

and classism and sexism have clipped our wings and our tongues and our imaginations; even if we know the literal and metaphorical violence Black people are up against daily; even if we know the straitjackets of stereotype and its consequences, we have sages among us who teach us how to think outside the proverbial box even as they know how to delineate the parameters of the box, who can imagine what the poet Robert Hayden called "something patterned, wild, and free," which is to say Black selves beyond the reach of the pernicious roadblocks to our full and flourishing personhood.

I am always watching for free Black men, in the public arena and up close, and I know them when I see them. I had a university colleague once who would proclaim out loud, "This is BORING!" in his meetings with his all-white colleagues talking infinitely about the supposed superiority of European culture. He didn't meet their arguments with measured reasoning, with footnotes. He didn't clench his jaw, clear his throat, sip from a lukewarm glass of water. No, he rejected the terms of their assertions and gave them not one second of his own considerable intellectual energy. He merely dismissed them. This thrilled and empowered me beyond measure: this man had said the emperor had no clothes! How liberating to say, *Maybe they're not that smart and maybe they're not that fascinating and maybe their worldview can be countered.*

The brother I see unabashedly kissing his son goodbye every morning at a nearby school drop-off is a free Black man to me. Most Black jazz musicians are free Black men, listening for their own strange, unprecedented, and historical selves in the sometimes powerfully nonrepresentational language of music. Free Black men who are quiet, free Black men who are loud. I invite you to imagine the free Black men in your communities. It is a very useful exercise.

Free Black men. Some of the things my father taught me: always carry "fuck you money" and keep some in the bank, no matter what, so that you have your own money on you so you can always walk away from the man, the job, the situation, and not have it cost you your health, your dignity, your life. This philosophy goes beyond the dime for the emergency phone call. The point was that no white person's job was worth your mental health. Period. My father taught me about always speaking up for what you knew was right even when no one in the room would sign on with you, because you never knew who would be listening, and someone was always listening. About learning to ignore fools, simply ignore them, reject their paradigm, render them irrelevant, even if they have power over your very livelihood. This is not always practical advice, but it is soul-saving. And even when you don't act according to that dictum, to have heard it stated is crucial and enabling. The freedom of mind I learned from him is that seeing yourself relative to the always-dominant paradigm is a soul-killing game, and that if we evaluate ourselves in terms of that paradigm we will always come up short and supplicating.

He saw his mother work, like most Black men. His mother was a righteous warrior who taught him things like memorizing badge numbers of Harlem police officers in the 1930s and '40s and then reporting them for their abuses against Black children. My father's first police encounter happened when he was eight. His mother organized a successful campaign against New York City newspapers to get them to stop identifying only Black alleged criminals by their race. His own father was a quieter man who taught my father much about kindness and decency, hard work and diligence, and honor. In their different ways, each taught him freedom.

I want my children to be free. What does that mean? How much worry is enough and what is the affective power of a mother's worry? I will continue this argument in a moment: the free Black men cannot exist without Black feminists. *Free* in this context doesn't just mean having accomplished the seemingly impossible. It doesn't just mean being outspoken. It means, to borrow from Langston Hughes, "free within ourselves" but in a way that is discernible and legible to those in our community.[55]

I am a Black mother of two Black sons. I exult in them, their accomplishments and happiness and struggles. And I worry about them so deeply it enters what sleep I have, from time to time, and I dream, when I am not exhausted, dream my worries for them.

Every Black mother I know is exhausted in her own way. I think every Black mother must dream her fears about our children. I cannot write my dreams, for fear they will come true if I speak them into form.

One friend tells me of a dream she had where she was flying in an old-fashioned twin plane with her teenage son. They were flying in tandem, until she was suddenly ejected from the plane seat and fell, fell, fell to the ocean below. She looked up and saw her son continue to fly while the pieces of her side of the plane broke off: wings, engine, body. He continued to fly the half plane, but she knew it could not support him. Her desperation was animal and wild. "I pushed my body through the air to try to reach him," she tells me. "And then the dream ended."

Or Black mothers are not dreaming, because we are so exhausted that the dream space is without language or image, just darkness. If Black children belong to us—and we need not be mothers, or fathers, or even Black for Black children to belong to us—a part of us is always vigilant, and always exhausted.

In spring, I listen to communities of birds from my New York window, high above any treetops. They are migrating birds, a friend tells me, and some have come from as far as South America. She tells me that such birds have two-chambered brains that allow them to sleep as they fly. This is what it means to sleep with one eye open. I feel there is no better metaphor for the never-rest of people who love and take responsibility for Black children. And especially for Black mothers.

I tell my sons, who are young men, and the young people they bring with them into our lives, to care for each other and themselves. I tell them, also, that they cannot solve every problem, nor are they responsible for all woes. No one is. You cannot unknow inequity. Perhaps the greatest

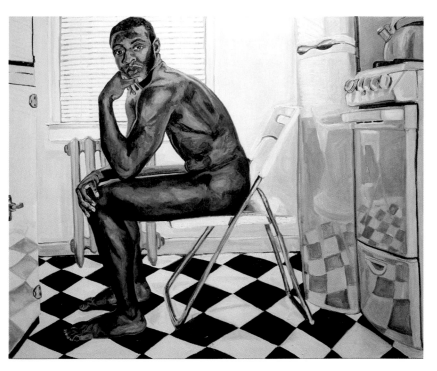

Jordan Casteel
Galen 2, 2014

triumph is to live to tell and bear witness to the struggles of others. To understand that blood ties are not the only ties that bind. They cannot be. Without communal care and sense of responsibility, and bearing witness, we cannot know that we will survive into the future. I hope that we are as Langston Hughes told us we must be, free within ourselves. But our freedom must be seized and reasserted every day.

I wish for our young people freedom of movement, of thought, of imagination. That is why the brilliance of our writers and artists is so crucial for them, to learn from and to call them into their own imagining and self-expression. And our tradition has an infinite supply of stories of ingenious survival and making a way out of no way. We do not yet know what a more just future looks like. We do not fully know what freedom feels like. It will take many forms. I wish also for our young people rest from the unending labor that is race work, and from the spectral anxiety that is part of what it is to be Black.

Peter Kunhardt's film *King in the Wilderness* chronicles the last year in the life of Martin Luther King, lonely as he leaves the ones he loves to do the work he must do and that he senses may bring him to his death. It is narrated by Dr. King's friends and associates from that time, now elders, who tell us about that year. They are not only elders, they are survivors. And we understand the profound sacrifice and loneliness that can accompany visionary leadership and righteous work, as well as feeling a deeper sense of King the human being and the ideals he and his generation-mates were serving.

My father is one of those people who worked with Dr. King and other civil rights leaders, bringing them to the White House to meet with President Johnson and advance the shared goals and hopes of that period. He was a young man in his early thirties, working as special counsel to the president in that short, potent stretch of American history.

In *King in the Wilderness*, my father is eighty-three. He leans forward into the camera when he speaks, eyebrows raised to open his face wide in urgency. "They discovered only after [King's] death that he was more radical than they actually knew," he says. "I don't think he wanted us to take anything other than all that we deserve. And that's what radicalism—in the best sense—is about: using the power that you have to transform the society for the better." My father is a lion in winter among his fellow wise warriors in the film, still making his case for our humanity, as has been his life's work and is now a bequest to our children.

Why do I end with my father in a film, when he is with us, and I have so many private memories of him imparting wisdom?

Because he was captured in a work of documentary art that lasts and carries on. It captures life force in its celluloid, or paper, or canvas, or digital files. It is not just for me or my children. It is for anyone within the sound of the movie's voice. None of us shall live forever. But art and knowledge and wisdom can.

Art and history are the indelibles. They outlive flesh. They offer us a compass or a lantern with which to move through the wilderness and allow us to imagine something different and better.

John Coltrane's eternal album *A Love Supreme* was made in one session in 1964, in the midst of the accruing violence of war and assassination. A refrain plays like the chanting Coltrane had come to understand in his religious practice, there is music, music, music, and no words. And after some minutes, we hear Coltrane's voice recorded over and over, rendering it more powerful and himself not alone, and making community as he sings "A love supreme, a love supreme, a love supreme, a love supreme."

What can the Black chant make happen? It sustains us. It is balm. It is remembrance. It is provocation. It is incantation. It is human. It is power.

The first time I heard this record I was nineteen years old in a college Black literature class, not new to jazz but new to such supreme transcendence. The students and professor sat together in a small seminar room and listened to the album all the way through without speaking. And the sound lifted us in ways we did not fully understand but knew had reached into our souls and asked us to be human together.

Almost all of the people in that room, Black and brilliant, have been dead for years. I remember them and carry what they gave me.

In his first book, *Dear John, Dear Coltrane*, Michael S. Harper made an inevitable-seeming juxtaposition of the refrain and Du Bois's account of seeing Black body parts sold after a lynching: "sex fingers toes / in the marketplace."[56] I can hear Harper's rich voice reading:

Why you so black?
cause I am

why you so funky?

cause I am

why you so black?

cause I am

why you so sweet?

cause I am

why you so black?

cause I am

a love supreme, a love supreme:

The poem and the song answer for me the questions of what we sing and what we say when we are seemingly forever in the knot of a history that will not let us be.

Dear John, Dear Coltrane was made right after King's trip to Memphis to support the striking sanitation workers, who carried signs that said, "I AM A MAN." Harper brought that plea for humanity into the poem, the voice of the artist Coltrane and the voice of everyday people asking to be treated as human.

The human connection has been all but gone in the last year of the global pandemic that has kept us apart from the people we love, the culture we need, and touch we crave, in a time when we most need to love and to grieve. Millions of

Betye Saar
Black Girl's Window, 1969

people are missing the dead they were unable to comfort in their final hours and be with when they passed, or ritualize after they died. Half of planet Earth had been sequestered for nearly eighteen months. If we think we can measure the effect of that right now, we are wrong. The losses have been disproportionately Black and brown.

But if we are overstimulated by the technology that brings images to us, we are also connected by it. The art, the ideas, the words, the exchanges that teach and inspire us are more widely available to us than ever before. The ability to organize on the ground has now been enhanced by the ability to organize virtually.

Artists make radical solutions all day long, soup from a stone, beauty from thin air. We see and try and discard and see again. We vision. We discard. We invent. We do it in the dark, we bring it into community. Artists continue to generate in a dangerous world that is nonetheless overflowing with life force and power. Creativity, making, and imagining animate Black self-determination with that which only culture can provide.

And people make movements and history with the force of creativity. The truly heroic drama of Black struggle is seen in the vivid figurative language of visionary leadership, the tableaux of fierce and proud resistance, the blazing beauty of people who survive indignities that might seem unbearable, the style and innovation with which Black people keep on stepping, offering countless examples to remind us of what has been overcome as well as to spark possibility for envisioning the new.

Sometimes the answers are not literal. Sometimes they take the form of human touch, of the love or encouragement that is transmitted in communities, or of the abstract space of possibility that is breath, carved out inside of us when we literally breathe to live and breathe to speak the truth. Artists are the visionaries who can help us imagine the unseen possibilities when we are faced with so much violence in what I fervently wish are the dying embers of an era of violent white supremacism, incivility, and hatred.

We Black people were largely brought to this soil in the category of property. In the eyes of the law we were three-fifths human. Out of this status, we became the seers who have continuously articulated the problem, the hope, and the possibility of America. We have expressed the core of what it is to be human and to aspire to better enact that humanity. I believe we have been able to do this because we have accessed near-ancestral knowledge and wisdom—for our enslaved progenitors are within reach of memory and lore, still, in our families—as well as the energy, courage, and new sight of the young people who so often catalyze our movements. There is no progress without generations working together. And there is no North Star without vigorous creativity to imagine it for us and mark where it lights the way.

Acknowledgments

I am now twice-grateful for my editor, Gretchen Young. Our second book together had a difficult birth and I am appreciative of her expert midwifery, brilliant editorial eye, and steadfast belief in what I have to offer. Thank you also to her wonderful colleagues at Grand Central. Faith Childs has encouraged my work every step of the way for over three decades. I am grateful to David Remnick for reading fast, saying yes, and along with his *New Yorker* colleagues, making the essay at the heart of this collection as good as it could be.

My colleagues at the Mellon Foundation, Michael Shattner, Ehsan Jami, and Julie Ehrlich, cleared the way many times over for me to find the time and space to write this book while attending to my job responsibilities. Josie Hodson and Martha Scott Burton were meticulous researchers who also brought me wonderful ideas for the artists I included in the book. Martha Scott was a crucial interlocutor for me as I made my choices, and she helped prepare the manuscript with great expertise, precision, and perseverance.

To the artists and poets included within, thank you for giving permission to include your work as part of the conversation and the reading experience of this book.

For my parents, thank you for the profound gift of raising me to be a race woman.

To my beloved family of friends, my village, I love you and cherish belonging to you, especially across the heightened distance of pandemic. These ideas have been nourished by our conversations.

To my writer friends who encouraged me, wrote with me remotely, exhorted me to write or told me, you never have to write another word in your life, thank you.

To my many students over the decades, I have learned so much from you and I write for you. Thank you.

To the elders, who lived through and taught us so much.

To the young ones, who continue to show us how it feels to be free.

Finally, to my two hearts, Solomon and Simon, this book would not exist without you to say it to. Your faith in me and love for me is everything in this world.

Notes

1. United States Census Bureau, American Community Survey Five Year Estimate.
2. Southern Poverty Law Center, "Whose Heritage? Public Symbols of the Confederacy," accessed May 3, 2021, https://www.splcenter .org/whose-heritage.
3. See Deirdre Benia Cooper Owens, *Medical Bondage: Race, Gender, and the Origins of American Gynecology* (Athens, GA: University of Georgia Press, 2018); Harriet A. Washington, *Medical Apartheid: The Dark History of Medical Experimentation on Black Americans from Colonial Times to the Present* (New York: Doubleday, 2006); and Dorothy E. Roberts, *Killing the Black Body: Race, Reproduction, and the Meaning of Liberty* (New York: Vintage Books, 1997).
4. Southern Poverty Law Center, Booth Gunter, and Jamie Kizzire, *Whose Heritage? Public Symbols of the Confederacy* (Montgomery, AL: Southern Poverty Law Center, 2016), https://www.splcenter.org /sites/default/files/com_whose_heritage.pdf.
5. Southern Poverty Law Center, "Whose Heritage? Public Symbols of the Confederacy."
6. Lucille Clifton and Charles H. Rowell, "An Interview with Lucille Clifton," *Callaloo* 22, no. 1 (1999): 57–58.
7. Debra McKinney, "Stone Mountain: A Monumental Dilemma," *The Intelligence Report*, Spring 2018, https://www.splcenter.org

/fighting-hate/intelligence-report/2018/stone-mountain-monu
mental-dilemma.

8. McKinney, "Stone Mountain."

9. Doreen St Félix, "Kara Walker's Next Act," *Vulture*, April 16, 2017, https://www.vulture.com/2017/04/kara-walker-after-a-subtlety .html.

10. Lucille Clifton, "in the inner city," in *The Collected Poems of Lucille Clifton 1965–2010*, eds. Kevin Young and Michael S. Glaser (Rochester, NY: BOA Editions, Ltd., 2012), 35.

11. Jonathan Holloway, "Yale's Narrative, and Yours," *Yale Alumni Magazine*, December 2015, https://yalealumnimagazine.com/arti cles/4171-yales-narrative-andyours.

12. Adrienne Su, "Personal History," Academy of American Poets, December 4, 2019, https://poets.org/poem/personal-history.

13. Jacob Stern, "Corey Menafee: Back to Work," *Yale Daily News*, November 14, 2016, https://features.yaledailynews.com/blog/2016 /11/14/corey-menafee-back-to-work/.

14. Elizabeth Fitzsousa, Nientara Anderson, and Anna Reisman, "'This Institution Was Never Meant for Me': The Impact of Institutional Historical Portraiture on Medical Students," *Journal of General Internal Medicine* 34, no. 12 (December 2019): 2738–39.

15. Adelaide M. Cromwell, *Unveiled Voices, Unvarnished Memories: The Cromwell Family in Slavery and Segregation, 1692–1972* (Columbia: University of Missouri Press, 2007), 148.

16. Alumni Records Office, Yale University, Records of Alumni from the Classes of 1701–1978 (RU 830), Manuscripts and Archives, Yale University Library.

17. Emily Hoffman and Isabel Polon, *Reflections on Coeducation: A Critical History of Women at Yale* (New Haven, CT: Yale University Library, 2010).

18. Jon Victor, Monica Wang, and Victor Wang, "More than 1,000 Gather in Solidarity," *Yale Daily News*, November 10, 2015, https://yaledailynews.com/blog/2015/11/10/more-than-1000-gather-in-solidarity/.

19. Elaine Lewinnek, "Social Studies Controversies in 1960s Los Angeles: Land of the Free, Public Memory, and the Rise of the New Right," *Pacific Historical Review* 84, no. 1 (2015): 57.

20. Joseph Moreau, "The Narrative 'Unravels,' 1961–1985: A Story in Three Parts," in *Schoolbook Nation: Conflicts over American History Textbooks from the Civil War to the Present* (Ann Arbor: University of Michigan Press, 2004), 291, 300.

21. Lewinnek, "Social Studies Controversies in 1960s Los Angeles," 63.

22. John Hope Franklin, *Mirror to America: The Autobiography of John Hope Franklin* (New York: Farrar, Straus and Giroux, 2013), 229–30.

23. Tony Kushner, *Angels in America: A Gay Fantasia on National Themes* (New York: Theatre Communications Group, 2013), 230.

24. Mandi Isaacs Jackson, "On Dixwell Avenue: Civil Rights and the Street," in *Model City Blues: Urban Space and Organized Resistance in New Haven* (Philadelphia: Temple University Press, 2008), 54, 71.

25. Mark Abraham et al., *Greater New Haven Community Index* (New Haven, CT: DataHaven, 2019), https://www.ctdatahaven.org/sites/ctdatahaven/files/DataHaven_GNH_Community_Index_2019.pdf.

26. United States Census Bureau.

27. Alice Walker, "Looking for Zora," in *In Search of Our Mothers' Gardens*, reprint (Orlando, FL: Harvest Books, 2003), 105, 115.

28. Zora Neale Hurston and Carla Kaplan, *Zora Neale Hurston: A Life in Letters* (New York: Anchor Books, 2003), 17.

29. Zora Neale Hurston, letter from Zora Neale Hurston to W. E. B. Du Bois, June 11, 1945, W. E. B. Du Bois Papers (MS 312), Special Collections and University Archives, University of Massachusetts Amherst Libraries.

30. W. E. B. Du Bois, letter from W. E. B. Du Bois to Zora Neale Hurston, July 11, 1945, W. E. B. Du Bois Papers (MS 312), Special Collections and University Archives, University of Massachusetts Amherst Libraries.

31. Toni Morrison, *Sula*, reprint (New York: Vintage International, 2004), 67–69.

32. June Jordan, "Who Look at Me," in *The Essential June Jordan*, ed. Jan Heller Levi and Christoph Keller (Port Townsend, WA: Copper Canyon Press, 2021), 6.

33. Gwendolyn Brooks, "the mother," in *The Essential Gwendolyn Brooks*, ed. Elizabeth Alexander (New York: Library of America, 2005), 2.

34. Toni Morrison, *Beloved*, reprint (New York: Vintage International, 2004), 6.

35. Frederick Douglass, *Narrative of the Life of Frederick Douglass: An American Slave, Written by Himself* (Boston: Anti-Slavery Office, 1845), 15.

36. Langston Hughes, "The Negro Artist and the Racial Mountain," *Nation*, June 23, 1926.

37. Chandra McCormick et al., "Louisiana Medley: The Social Justice Photography of Chandra McCormick and Keith Calhoun," Artist Talk, Harvard Art Museums, November 6, 2019, video, https://youtu.be/a4iSAwjBtnw.

38. James Ridgeway, "God's Own Warden," *Mother Jones*, July/August 2011, https://www.motherjones.com/politics/2011/07/burl-cain-angola-prison/.

39. Deborah Luster and C. D. Wright, *One Big Self: Prisoners of Louisiana* (Santa Fe, NM: Twin Palms Publishing, 2003).

40. The Kitchen Sisters, "After Mother's Murder, Artist Photographs Prisoners," *All Things Considered*, June 30, 2010, NPR, https://www.npr.org/2010/06/30/128212442/after-mothers-murder-artist-photographs-prisoners.

41. Katie Rose Quandt and James Ridgeway, "At Angola Prison, Getting Sick Can Be a Death Sentence," *In These Times*, December 2016, https://www.inthesetimes.com/features/angola-prison-health care-abuse-investigation.html.

42. See, for example, Mary Frances Berry, "'Reckless Eyeballing': The Matt Ingram Case and the Denial of African American Sexual Freedom," *The Journal of African American History* 93, no. 2 (2008): 223–34.

43. On the disproportionate representation of incarcerated Black and Latino men restricted to solitary confinement, see, for example, Andrea C. Armstrong, "Race, Prison Discipline, and the Law," *UC Irvine Law Review* 5, no. 759 (2015): 759–82.

44. Priscilla Frank, "Wrongfully Trapped in Solitary Confinement, Herman Wallace Built His Dream House," *Huffington Post*, July 26, 2016, https://www.huffpost.com/entry/in-solitary-confinement-for-a-crime-he-didnt-commit-herman-wallace-built-his-dream-house_n_579651a3e4b0d3568f840274.

45. Alvin Borgquist, letter from Alvin Borgquist to W. E. B. Du Bois, April 3, 1905, W. E. B. Du Bois Papers (MS 312), Special Collections and University Archives, University of Massachusetts Amherst Libraries.

46. Du Bois, letter from W. E. B. Du Bois to Alvin Borgquist, April 11, 1905, W. E. B. Du Bois Papers (MS 312), Special Collections and University Archives, University of Massachusetts Amherst Libraries.

47. Rochelle Olson et al., "Medical Expert: 'In a Vise,' George Floyd Did Everything He Could as He Struggled to Breathe," *Star*

Tribune, April 9, 2021, https://www.startribune.com/medical-expert-in-a-vise-george-floyd-did-everything-he-could-as-he-struggled-to-breathe/600043818/.

48. Leila Fadel, "Voices from the Trial Over George Floyd's Killing," *All Things Considered*, April 3, 2021, NPR, https://www.npr.org/2021/04/03/984145332/voices-from-the-trial-over-george-floyds-killing.

49. Laurel Wamsley, "George Floyd's Brother Testifies in Derek Chauvin Trial," April 12, 2021, NPR, https://www.npr.org/sections/trial-over-killing-of-george-floyd/2021/04/12/986508546/watch-george-floyds-brother-testifies-in-derek-chauvin-trial.

50. Julia Halperin, "A Developer Censored a 'Divisive' Art Billboard Saying 'There Are Black People in the Future'—Then the Backlash Began," Artnet News, April 6, 2018, https://news.artnet.com/art-world/billboard-censored-pittsburgh-1260494.

51. Brooks, "I Am A Black," in *The Essential Gwendolyn Brooks*, 128.

52. Audre Lorde, "A Litany for Survival," in *The Collected Poems of Audre Lorde* (New York: W. W. Norton & Company, 2000), 256.

53. Lucille Clifton, "won't you celebrate with me," in *The Book of Light* (Port Townsend, WA: Copper Canyon Press, 1993), 25.

54. Mike Ives and Maria Cramer, "Black Army Officer Pepper-Sprayed in Traffic Stop Accuses Officers of Assault," *The New York Times*, April 10, 2021, https://www.nytimes.com/2021/04/10/us/caron-nazario-windsor-police-virginia.html.

55. Hughes, "The Negro Artist and the Racial Mountain."

56. Michael S. Harper, "Dear John, Dear Coltrane," in *Songlines in Michaeltree: New and Collected Poems* (Champaign: University of Illinois Press, 2002), 25.

Credits

IMAGES

Jennifer Packer, *Blessed Are Those Who Mourn (Breonna! Breonna!)*, 2020
Oil on canvas
118 x 172½ in. (299.7 x 438.2 cm)
Artwork © Jennifer Packer, courtesy of Sikkema Jenkins & Co. and
  Corvi-Mora.

Lorna Simpson, *Thin Bands* (detail), 2019
Ink and screenprint on gessoed fiberglass
Unique
108 x 96 x 1⅜ in. (274.3 x 243.8 x 3.5 cm)
© Lorna Simpson. Courtesy the artist and Hauser & Wirth. Photo:
  James Wang.

Glenn Ligon, *Untitled (I Am A Man)*, 1988
Oil and enamel on canvas
40 x 25 in. (101.6 x 63.5 cm)
Collection of National Gallery of Art, Washington.
© Glenn Ligon. Courtesy of the artist, Hauser & Wirth, New York,
  Regen Projects, Los Angeles, Thomas Dane Gallery, London, and
  Chantal Crousel, Paris. Digital image courtesy National Gallery of
  Art, Washington.

Kara Walker, *The Jubilant Martyrs of Obsolescence and Ruin*, 2015
Cut paper on wall
165.375 x 698.875 in. (420 x 1775 cm)
Artwork © Kara Walker, courtesy of Sikkema Jenkins & Co. and Sprüth
   Magers.

Mary Sibande, *The Reign*, 2010
Life-size fiberglass bodycast, life-size fiberglass horse, steel, and cotton textile
118 x 79 in. (330 x 201 cm)
© Mary Sibande. Courtesy of the artist and Kavi Gupta.

Robert Pruitt, *Up, Up, in the Upper Room*, 2012
Fabric dye, charcoal, and conté pastels
72 x 48 in. (182.9 x 121.9 cm)
© Robert Pruitt. Courtesy of the artist and Koplin Del Rio Gallery.

Amy Sherald, *What's precious inside of him does not care to be known by the
   mind in ways that diminish its presence (All American)*, 2017
Oil on canvas
54 x 43 x 2.5 in. (137.2 x 109.2 x 6.4 cm)
© Amy Sherald. Courtesy the artist and Hauser & Wirth.

Frank Stewart, *St. Louis Cemetery II*, 1980
© Frank Stewart. Courtesy of the artist.

Kerry James Marshall, *Souvenir II*, 1997
Acrylic, collage, and glitter on unstretched canvas banner
108 x 156 in. (274.3 x 396.2 cm)
© Kerry James Marshall. Courtesy of the artist and Jack Shainman
   Gallery, New York.

Dawoud Bey, *Martina and Rhonda*, Chicago, IL, 1993
Six dye diffusion transfer prints (Polaroid)
Overall (in-situ): 48 x 60 in. (121.9 x 152.4 cm); frame (each): 30¾ x 23 x 2 in. (78.1 x 58.4 x 5.1 cm); overall (framed): 61½ x 69 x 2 in. (156.2 x 175.3 x 5.1 cm)
© Dawoud Bey. Courtesy: Sean Kelly, New York.

Charles White, *Banner for Willie J.*, 1976
Oil on canvas
58¼ x 50⅛ in. (148 x 127.3 cm)
© The Charles White Archives. Courtesy of The Charles White Archives.

Elizabeth Catlett, *The Torture of Mothers*, 1970
Lithograph
15 x 22¼ in. (38.1 x 56.52 cm)
The University of Iowa Stanley Museum of Art. Museum purchase, 2006.61.
© 2021 Catlett Mora Family Trust / Licensed by VAGA at Artists Rights Society (ARS), NY.

Chandra McCormick, *Daddy'O, The Oldest Inmate in Angola State Penitentiary*, 2004
© 2004 Chandra McCormick. Courtesy of the artist.

Deborah Luster, *Eddie M. "Fat" Coco Jr., Transylvania, Louisiana*, March 8, 2002
Gelatin silver print on aluminum
5 x 3¹⁵/₁₆ in. (12.7 x 10 cm)
National Gallery of Art, Washington. Gift of Julia J. Norrell, in Honor of Claude Simard and the 25th Anniversary of Photography at the National Gallery of Art.

© Deborah Luster. Courtesy of the artist and Jack Shainman Gallery, New York. Digital image courtesy National Gallery of Art, Washington.

jackie sumell, *Herman Wallace's Conference Room*, 2008
© jackie sumell. Courtesy of the artist.

Jordan Casteel, *Galen 2*, 2014
Oil on canvas
72 x 84 in. (182.9 x 213.4 cm)
© Jordan Casteel. Courtesy of Casey Kaplan, New York. Private Collection.

Renée Cox, *Chillin' with Liberty*, 1998
CibaChrome Print
60 x 48 in. (152.4 x 121.9 cm)
© Renée Cox. Courtesy of the artist.

Robert Pruitt, *Untitled (Male Celestial Body)*, 2016
Conté, pastel, colored pencil, and charcoal on tea dyed paper
50 x 38 in. (127 x 96.5 cm)
© Robert Pruitt. Courtesy of the artist and Koplin Del Rio Gallery.

Betye Saar, *Black Girl's Window*, 1969
Mixed media
35¾ x 18 x 1½ in. (90.8 x 45.7 x 3.8 cm)
The Museum of Modern Art, New York. The Modern Women's Fund and Committee on Painting and Sculpture Funds.
© 2021 Betye Saar. Digital Image © The Museum of Modern Art / Licensed by SCALA / Art Resource, NY.

TEXTS

About the Author

Elizabeth Alexander is a prize-winning *New York Times* bestselling author, renowned American poet, educator, scholar, and cultural advocate. Among the fourteen books she has authored or coauthored, *American Sublime* was a finalist for the Pulitzer Prize in Poetry in 2006 and her memoir, *The Light of the World*, was a finalist for the Pulitzer Prize in Biography and the National Book Critics Circle Award in 2015. Other works include *Crave Radiance: New and Selected Poems 1990–2010* (2010), *Power and Possibility: Essays, Reviews, Interviews* (2007), *The Black Interior: Essays* (2004), *Antebellum Dream Book* (2001), *Body of Life* (1996), and *The Venus Hottentot* (1990). She has been awarded the Jackson Poetry Prize, the John Simon Guggenheim Memorial Foundation Fellowship, the George Kent Award, the National Endowment for the Arts Fellowship, and three Pushcart Prizes for Poetry. Notably, Dr. Alexander composed and delivered "Praise

Song for the Day" for the 2009 inauguration of President Barack Obama.

Dr. Alexander is president of the Andrew W. Mellon Foundation, the nation's largest funder of the arts, culture, and humanities. She is chancellor emeritus of the Academy of American Poets, a member of the American Academy of Arts and Sciences, serves on the Pulitzer Prize Board, and codesigned the Art for Justice Fund. Over the course of her career in education, she has held distinguished professorships at Smith College, Columbia University, and Yale University, where she taught for fifteen years and chaired the Department of African American Studies.